The Tyndale Old Test

W9-BBX-655

General Editor:
Professor D. J. Wiseman, O.B.E., M.A., D.Lit., F.B.A.,
F.S.A.

NAHUM, HABAKKUK
and ZEPHANIAH

NAHUM, HABAKKUK and ZEPHANIAH

AN INTRODUCTION AND COMMENTARY

by

DAVID W. BAKER, A.B., M.C.S., M.PHIL., PH.D.

*Associate Professor of Old Testament and Hebrew,
Ashland Theological Seminary, Ohio*

INTER-VARSITY PRESS
LEICESTER, ENGLAND
DOWNERS GROVE, ILLINOIS, USA

Inter-Varsity Press
38 De Montfort Street, Leicester LE1 7GP, England
P.O. Box 1400, Downers Grove, Illinois 60515, U.S.A.

©*1988 David W. Baker*

Inter-Varsity Press, England is the book-publishing division of the Universities and Colleges Christian Fellowship (formerly Inter-Varsity Fellowship), a student movement linking Christion Unions in universities and colleges throughout the United Kingdom and the Republic of Ireland, and a member movement of the International Fellowship of Evangelical Students. For information about local and national activities write to UCCF, 38 De Montfort Street, Leicester LE1 7GP.

InterVarsity Press, U.S.A., is the book-publishing division of InterVarsity Christian Fellowship, a student movement active on campus at hundreds of universities, colleges and schools of nursing. For information about local and regional activities, write Public Relations Dept., InterVarsity Christian Fellowship, 6400 Schroeder Rd., P.O. Box 7895, Madison, WI 53707-7895.

Distributed in Canada through InterVarsity Press, 860 Denison St., Unit 3, Markham, Ontario L3R 4H1, Canada.

Text set in Great Britain by Input Typesetting Ltd., London SW19
Printed in the United States of America
UK ISBN 0-8511-644-2 (cloth)
UK ISBN 0-8511-845-3 (paperback)
USA ISBN 0-8308-1427-2 (cloth)
USA ISBN 0-87784-249-3 (paperback)
USA ISBN 0-87784-880-7 (set of Tyndale Old Testament Commentaries, cloth)
USA ISBN 0-87784-280-9 (set of Tyndale Old Testament Commentaries, paperback)

British Library Cataloguing ain Publication Data

Nahum, Habakkuk, Zephaniah.——(The
  Tyndale Old Testament commentaries).
  1. Bible. O.T. Nahum, Critical studies
  2. Bible. O.T. Habakkuk - Commentaries
  3. Bible. O.T. Zephaniah - Commentaries
  I. Baker, David W. (David Weston),
  II. Series
  224'.9406

Library of Congress Cataloging-in-Publication Data
Baker, David W. (David Weston), 1950-
  Nahum, Habakkuk, Zephaniah : an introduction and commentary / by
David W. Baker.
    p. cm. – (Tyndale Old Testament commentaries)
    Bibliography: p.
    ISBN 0-8308-1427-2 (U.S.). ISBN 0-87784-249-3 (U.S. : pbk.)
    1. Bible. O.T. Nahum–Commentaries. 2. Bible. O.T. Habakkuk—
-Commentaries. 3. Bible. O.T. Zephaniah–Commentaries. I. Title.
II. Series.
BS 1625.3.B34 1988
224'.9–dc19

                                                                88-9360
                                                                CIP

15	14	13	12	11	10	9	8	7	6	5	4	3	2
99	98	97	96	95	94	93	92	91	90	89			

GENERAL PREFACE

THE aim of this series of *Tyndale Old Testament Commentaries*, as it was in the companion volumes on the New Testament, is to provide the student of the Bible with a handy, up-to-date commentary on each book, with the primary emphasis on exegesis. Major critical questions are discussed in the introductions and additional notes, while undue technicalities have been avoided.

In this series individual authors are, of course, free to make their own distinct contributions and express their own point of view on all debated issues. Within the necessary limits of space they frequently draw attention to interpretations which they themselves do not hold but which represent the stated conclusions of sincere fellow Christians.

The books of Nahum, Habakkuk and Zephaniah cover an important but turbulent epoch in the history of Israel in which prophets warned of coming judgment if Israel refused to turn back to God from her apostasy and to practise effective social justice. This culminated in the fall of Jerusalem in 587 BC and in the exile in Babylon.

In the Old Testament in particular no single English translation is adequate to reflect the original text. The version on which these three commentaries are based is the New International Version, but other translations are frequently referred to as well, and on occasion the author supplies his own. Where necessary, words are transliterated in order to help the reader who is unfamiliar with Hebrew to identify the precise word under discussion.

It is assumed throughout that the reader will have ready access to one, or more, reliable rendering of the Bible in English.

Interest in the meaning and message of the Old Testament continues undiminished and it is hoped that this series will thus further the systematic study of the revelation of God and his will and ways as seen in these records. It is the prayer of the editor and publisher, as of the authors, that these books will help many to understand, and to respond to, the Word of God today.

D. J. WISEMAN

CONTENTS

NAHUM

HABAKKUK

CONTENTS

ZEPHANIAH

AUTHOR'S PREFACE

WHEN travelling westwards across the American Great Plains, the Rocky Mountains in the far distance seem relatively minor and insignificant. As one eventually enters them, however, one is confronted at every turn with the power and beauty of these masterpieces of God's handiwork. The same experience of wonder and majesty is felt in approaching the 'minor' prophets, which are only minor in word count, but are often 'major' in literary quality and theological relevance. As one can only hope to enjoy a fraction of the alpine splendour, so one realizes that much of the potential of the prophets will also lie untapped. In both cases, one hopes at least to have touched on the most meaningful and exciting vistas of Nahum, Habakkuk and Zephaniah.

For the privilege of making this journey I thank Professor D. J. Wiseman. His willingness to let me make the trip and his guidance along the way are much appreciated. For patient editorial leading I thank the Inter-Varsity Press and its staff. My deepest appreciation and love go to Morven for her constant support and encouragement. Little did she realize when she repeated Ruth's vow to accompany Naomi what paths God had in store.

DAVID W. BAKER

CHIEF ABBREVIATIONS

Bible translations and versions

AV	Authorized Version (King James), 1611.
BHS	A. Alt *et al.* (eds.), *Biblica Hebraica Stuttgartensia* (Deutsche Bibelstiftung Stuttgart, 1967/77).
DSS	Dead Sea Scrolls.
JB	Jerusalem Bible, 1966.
LXX	The Septuagint (Greek version of the Old Testament).
MT	Massoretic Text.
NEB	New English Bible, 1970.
NIV	New International Version, 1973, 1978, 1984.
NJB	New Jerusalem Bible, 1985.
RSV	Revised Standard Version, 1952.
Syr.	Syriac.
Vulg.	Vulgate.

Other reference works

ANET	J. B. Pritchard, *Ancient Near Eastern Texts Relating to the Old Testament* (Princeton University Press, ²1955; ³1969).
BDB	F. Brown, S. R. Driver and C. A. Briggs, *Hebrew and English Lexicon of the Old Testament* (Clarendon Press, 1906).
G-K	Gesenius-Kautzsch, *Hebrew Grammar*, ET, 1910.
IBD	J. D. Douglas *et al.* (eds.), *The Illustrated Bible Dictionary*, 3 vols. (IVP, 1980).
IDBS	K. Crim *et al.* (eds.), *The Interpreter's Dictionary of the Bible*, Supplementary volume (Abingdon Press, 1976).
NBD	J. D. Douglas *et al.* (eds.), *The New Bible Dictionary* (IVP, ²1982).
POTT	D. J. Wiseman (ed.), *Peoples of Old Testament Times* (Oxford University Press, 1973).

CHIEF ABBREVIATIONS

Journals

CBQ	*Catholic Biblical Quarterly.*
JBL	*Journal of Biblical Literature.*
JNES	*Journal of Near Eastern Studies.*
JR	*Journal of Religion.*
OTS	*Oudtestamentlische Studien.*
VT	*Vetus Testamentum.*
ZAW	*Zeitschrift für die alttestamentliche Wissenschaft.*

SELECT BIBLIOGRAPHIES

Commentaries and works on Nahum

Cathcart   K. J. Cathcart, *Nahum in the Light of Northwest Semitic* (Pontifical Biblical Institute, 1973).

Coggins   R. J. Coggins, ' "In Wrath Remember Mercy" – A Commentary on the Book of Nahum' in R. J. Coggins and S. P. Re'emi, *Israel Among the Nations*, International Theological Commentary (Eerdmans/Handsel Press, 1985).

Craigie   P. C. Craigie, *Twelve Prophets* 1, Daily Study Bible (Westminster/St Andrew Press, 1984).

Eaton   J. H. Eaton, *Obadiah, Nahum, Habakkuk and Zephaniah*, Torch Bible Commentaries (SCM Press, 1961).

Keil   C. F. Keil, 'Nahum' in *The Twelve Minor Prophets* 2, trans. J. Martin (Eerdmans, 1949).

Laetsch   T. F. C. Laetsch, *Bible Commentary: The Minor Prophets* (Concordia, 1956).

Maier   W. A. Maier, *The Book of Nahum* (Concordia, 1959).

Rudolph   W. Rudolph, *Micha – Nahum – Habakuk – Zephanja*, Kommentar zum Alten Testament (GVGM, 1975).

G. A. Smith   G. A. Smith, *The Book of the Twelve Prophets*, The Expositor's Bible (A. C. Armstrong, ²1901).

J. M. P. Smith   J. M. P. Smith, 'Nahum' in J. M. P. Smith, W. H. Ward and J. A. Bewer, *A Critical and Exegetical Commentary on Micah, Zephaniah, Nahum, Habakkuk, Obadiah and Joel*, International Critical Commentary (T. & T. Clark/Scribners, 1911).

R. L. Smith   R. L. Smith, *Micah – Malachi*, Word Biblical Commentary (Word Books, 1984).

Watts   J. D. W. Watts, *The Books of Joel, Obadiah, Jonah, Nahum, Habakkuk and Zephaniah*, Cambridge

Bible Commentary (Cambridge University Press, 1975).

Commentaries and works on Habakkuk

Armerding   C. E. Armerding, *Habakkuk* in F. E. Gaebelein (ed.), *The Expositor's Bible Commentary* 7 (Zondervan, 1985).

Brownlee   W. H. Brownlee, *The Midrash Pesher of Habbakuk* (Scholars Press, 1979).

Craigie   P. C. Craigie, *Twelve Prophets* 2, Daily Study Bible (Westminster/St Andrew Press, 1985).

Eaton   J. H. Eaton, *Obadiah, Nahum, Habakkuk and Zephaniah*, Torch Bible Commentaries (SCM Press, 1961).

Gowan   D. E. Gowan, *The Triumph of Faith in Habakkuk* (John Knox Press, 1976).

Jöcken   P. Jöcken, *Das Buch Habakuk: Darstellung der Geschichte seiner kritischen Erforschung mit einer eigenen Beurteilung* (Peter Hanstein, 1977).

Keil   C. F. Keil, 'Habakkuk' in *The Twelve Minor Prophets* 2, trans. J. Martin (Eerdmans, 1949).

Laetsch   T. F. C. Laetsch, *Bible Commentary: The Minor Prophets* (Concordia, 1956).

Lloyd-Jones   D. M. Lloyd-Jones, *From Fear to Faith* (IVF, 1953; republished in *Faith Tried and Triumphant*, IVP, 1987).

Rudolph   W. Rudolph, *Micha – Nahum – Habakuk – Zephanja* (GVGM, 1975).

G. A. Smith   G. A. Smith, *The Book of the Twelve Prophets*, The Expositor's Bible (A. C. Armstrong/Hodder & Stoughton, 1898).

R. L. Smith   R. L. Smith, *Micah – Malachi*, Word Biblical Commentary (Word Books, 1984).

Ward   W. H. Ward, 'Habakkuk' in J. M. P. Smith, W. H. Ward and J. A. Bewer, *A Critical and Exegetical Commentary on Micah, Zephaniah, Nahum, Habakkuk, Obadiah and Joel*, International Critical Commentary (T. & T. Clark/Scribners, 1911).

Watts   J. D. W. Watts, *The Books of Joel, Obadiah, Jonah, Nahum, Habakkuk and Zephaniah*, Cambridge

Bible Commentary (Cambridge University Press, 1975).

Commentaries and works on Zephaniah

Achtemeier E. Achtemeier, *Nahum – Malachi* (John Knox Press, 1986).

Craigie P. C. Craigie, *Twelve Prophets* 2, Daily Study Bible (Westminster/St Andrew Press, 1985).

Eaton J. H. Eaton, *Obadiah, Nahum, Habakkuk and Zephaniah*, Torch Bible Commentaries (SCM Press, 1961).

Irsigler H. Irsigler, *Gottesgericht und Jahwetag: Die Komposition Zef 1, 1–2, 3, untersucht auf der Grundlage der Literarkritik des Zefanjabuch* (EOS-Verlag, 1977).

Kapelrud A. S. Kapelrud, *The Message of the Prophet Zephaniah* (Universitetsforlaget, 1975).

Keil C. F. Keil, 'Zephaniah' in *The Twelve Minor Prophets* 2, trans. J. Martin (Eerdmans, 1949).

Laetsch T. F. C. Laetsch, *Bible Commentary: The Minor Prophets* (Concordia, 1956).

Rudolph W. Rudolph, *Micha – Nahum – Habakuk – Zephanja* (GVGM, 1975).

Sabottka L. Sabottka, *Zephanja* (Pontifical Biblical Institute, 1972).

G. A. Smith G. A. Smith, *The Book of the Twelve Prophets*, The Expositor's Bible (Doubleday, 1929).

J. M. P. Smith J. M. P. Smith, 'Zephaniah' in J. M. P. Smith, W. H. Ward and J. A. Bewer, *A Critical and Exegetical Commentary on Micah, Zephaniah, Nahum, Habakkuk, Obadiah and Joel*, International Critical Commentary (T. & T. Clark/Scribners, 1911).

R. L. Smith R. L. Smith, *Micah – Malachi*, Word Biblical Commentary (Word Books, 1984).

Watts J. D. W. Watts, *The Books of Joel, Obadiah, Jonah, Nahum, Habakkuk and Zephaniah*, Cambridge Bible Commentary (Cambridge University Press, 1975).

NAHUM

INTRODUCTION

I. THE MAN

THE name 'Nahum' means most probably 'comfort' or 'reassurance'. It occurs only in the first verse of this book and in Luke 3:25 (of an ancestor of Jesus, though different people are meant). It occurs more frequently in extra-biblical sources, and in the Bible the related 'Nehemiah' is common. Nothing is known of the Nahum associated with this prophecy except that he was an Elkoshite, coming from the town or region of Elkosh.

Several suggestions have been made as to the location of Elkosh. One links it to *al-Qosh*, 50 km north of modern Mosul. This identification is relatively recent and has not attracted much scholarly support since there is no convincing evidence from within the book itself of an Assyrian origin.[1] Jerome identified Elkosh with a small town in northern Galilee, and a later tradition in the area links Nahum with the 'village of Nahum', Capernaum. A more likely identification is with Beit-Jebrin in Judah. This is preferred since the northern kingdom of Israel was already in exile, effectively precluding an Israelite site, and no message of hope for restoration is given, making an exilic location and date difficult.[2]

II. THE TIME

There is no explicit date in the book of Nahum, but internal evidence suggests a date in the mid-seventh century BC. The Assyrian empire is strong, which indicates a date prior to 612

[1] A. S. van der Woude, in his article 'The Book of Nahum: A Letter Written in Exile', *OTS* 20 (1977), pp. 100–127, argues for an Assyrian background to the prophecy.

[2] Rudolph, p. 149, sees a possible Edomite connection in the name being *'ēl qôš*, 'the God *Qoš*' ', an Edomite deity.

BC, when Nineveh fell.[1] This fall is the substance of the prophecy. The strength of the Assyrian empire indicates a date prior to the death of Ashurbanipal (668–627 BC). Subsequently the nation rapidly declined before the ascendancy of Babylonia.

The clearest historical reference in the book is to the fall of Thebes (modern Karnak or Luxor, some 530 km upstream from Cairo; 3:8), which fell to Assyria in 663 BC. This was in spite of her call to neighbouring countries for assistance against the attacker.[2] Wellhausen argued that this description must have come soon after the event portrayed.[3] Within this time period, the harshest Assyrian domination of Judah was under Manasseh (687/6–672 BC), while the Assyrian yoke was dislodged under Josiah (640–609 BC). If the events in 2:2 look forward in time, they would then have occurred in the time of Manasseh, but if they reflect an accomplished event, they would have been penned under Josiah. Confidence in the Assyrian downfall, such as found in this prophecy, could have sparked off Manasseh's rebellion (2 Ch. 33:14–16) of about 652–648 BC.[4] The fall of Assyria, and of Nineveh in particular, was brought about by a military coalition of her neighbours, the Babylonians and Medes, starting from the death of Ashurbanipal in 627 BC and culminating with the destruction of Nineveh in 612 BC.[5] Some have proposed a post-612 BC date for Nahum, arguing that it was composed as a liturgical response to Nineveh's fall, but this proposal has not met with much acceptance. However, while not having a cultic origin, the book could well have had a cultic use after the events foretold in it came to pass. It would then serve as a vindication of Yahweh's power and justice.

[1] *ANET*, p. 304. For a discussion of the Assyrian capital, see D. J. Wiseman, 'Nineveh', *IBD*, pp. 1089–1092.

[2] See *ANET*, p. 295, ii; J. Bright, *A History of Israel* (SCM Press/Westminster, ³1980), p. 311.

[3] Cited by Maier, p. 36.

[4] For a recent discussion of date, see D. L. Christensen, 'The Acrostic of Nahum Reconsidered', *ZAW* 87 (1975), pp. 27–29, esp. p. 29, for this last point.

[5] See *ANET*, pp. 304–305; Bright, *History of Israel*, pp. 315–316.

III. THE BOOK AND ITS STRUCTURE

Nahum is the seventh member of 'the twelve' or the Minor Prophets. All canonical traditions place it before Habakkuk and all place it after Micah, except the LXX, where it follows Jonah.

The book is in the form of an oracle (1:1). The Hebrew word translated 'oracle' (*maśśā'*) comes from the root *nś'*. It occurs in the Old Testament with two different meanings. Whether the two meanings arose from a common original or whether two originally separate words resulted in the same lexical form is not clear. In several cases the regular meaning of the root as 'lift, carry' is evident in meanings such as 'load, burden' (*e.g.* 2 Ki. 5:17; 2 Ch. 35:3; Je. 17:21). This use is extended to include not only physical carrying but any 'hardship' (*e.g.* Nu. 11:11; Dt. 1:12). It has been suggested that it is this connotation of a 'burden' or hardship which is used when the word begins an oracle (*cf.* AV), usually of judgment. The problem with this is that not every occurrence of the word is in the context of judgment (*cf.* Zc. 12:1). The interpretation of the word as a homonym with the technical meaning 'oracle, pronouncement' fits better in this prophetic context (*cf.*, *e.g.*, Ezk. 12:10; Hab. 1:1; Zc. 9:1; Mal. 1:1). The fact that there are two distinct meanings for the same form explains the punning word play found in Jeremiah 23:33–38.[1]

The prophecy concerns the destruction of the Assyrian oppressor and the resulting relief for the oppressed Judah. The literary forms and stylistic devices used to express this message are varied. The first section is a psalm of descriptive praise or a hymn which praises God for his character (1:2–8). There then follows a court scene. Here alternating verdicts of judgment and acquittal are given to Assyria and Judah respectively (1:12 – 2:2). There is vivid description of siege and battle (2:1, 3–10; 3:2–3), as well as a dirge or lament (3:1). The writer uses metaphor and simile in extended passages (2:11–13; 3:4–7, 15–17) as well as in individual verses (*e.g.* 1:10, 13; 2:7; 3:12, 13). He also uses irony (3:1, 14). All these elements work to bring about the aim of the prophecy, that

---

[1] See S. Erlandsson, *The Burden of Babylon: A Study of Isaiah 13:2 – 14:23* (CWK Gleerup, 1970), pp. 64–65; W. McKane, '*Massa*' in Jeremiah 23, 33–40', in J. A. Emerton (ed.), *Prophecy: Essays Presented to George Fohrer on his Sixty-Fifth Birthday, 6 September, 1980* (W. de Gruyter, 1980), pp. 35–54.

is to cause a change in the hearers. It is doubtful whether the audience was Nineveh herself, since the Old Testament contains only one record of a prophecy actually addressed to people other than Israel (Jon. 3:4). This prophecy was probably given to encourage Judah to believe that the tyranny under which she lived would have an end.

The major literary problem of the book concerns the structure of the hymn in the first chapter. The question turns on the existence and extent of an acrostic, where each line begins with the next letter of the alphabet. Examples of this form are found in the Psalms (*e.g.* Ps. 119) and Lamentations. Being first suggested during the last century as regards Nahum, it has now become widely accepted that at least some, if not all, of the alphabet is included in the acrostic.[1] However, in order to present a complete alphabet, verses have to be radically reconstructed, usually without any manuscript or versional evidence. Even the more conservative proposal that half of the Hebrew alphabet (*'–k*) governs the structure of 1:2–8 requires emendations in four of the eleven lines concerned, yet none of these lines are incomprehensible as they now stand. In other words, the only motivation for change is for the text to fit to a pattern which theoretically arose from the text, making the argumentation circular.

The subjective nature of conjectural emendation, even in such a relatively conservative way as proposed by Christensen,[2] is not without its critics. As J. M. P. Smith wrote, 'by proceedings like those, any poem might be transformed into an acrostic',[3] while G. A. Smith noted that 'to have produced good or poetical Hebrew is not conclusive proof of having recovered the original'.[4] While originally there might very possibly have been a half acrostic, or even a whole one, we cannot find either in the present text. Whether the acrostic existed or not is of importance for literary form, but not for the meaning and content of the prophecy itself. While its existence could provide objective evidence of a new text section starting in 1:9, this is shown anyway by the change in grammatical form from the third person, talking *about* God in 1:2–8, to the second person, talking *to* someone about God in 1:9–11.

---

[1] See Christensen, 'Acrostic of Nahum', pp. 17–19, for a history of the discussion up to 1975.

[2] *Ibid.*, pp. 21–22.   [3] J. M. P. Smith, p. 309.   [4] G. A. Smith, p. 82.

IV. THE MESSAGE

The message of Nahum concerns God's character and his relationship to the world, not only to his own people but also to those who do not even acknowledge him. The hymn at the outset of the book (1:2–8) sets the context of the whole prophecy. Yahweh is jealous of his unique position as God and visits judicial vengeance upon those who oppose him and oppress his people (1:2). While he shows patience by at times delaying punishment, he is just and his righteous demands must ultimately be met or judgment will follow (1:3). This does not exclude God's own people, either Israel or the church, from judgment. What God desires is not a position or relationship which is assumed by some past action on the part of God, whether Sinai or Calvary, but a continued response of trust and reliance on God (1:7).

The author is not expressing some personal feeling of vindication over some hurt by the oppressor, nor even a nationalistic chauvinism that pagan nations must be punished. Rather, Yahweh is applying his universal standard against evil, no matter who is responsible (*cf.* Am. 1:3 – 2:16). Even though God has chosen Assyria to act as his instrument of punishment against the rebellious and recalcitrant Israel (Is. 7:17; 10:5–6), he holds that nation corporately responsible for the excesses and atrocities committed in fulfilling this role (Is. 10:7–19; *cf.* Zp. 2:14–15).

There might be concern that Nahum is unfairly one-sided in castigating a foreign power while not censuring the evil of his own people. This is not necessarily the case. In some collections of prophetic oracles the two notes of judgment and hope are preached together (*e.g.* Isaiah; Hosea). In others either judgment or hope is presented to the virtual exclusion of the other (*cf.* Obadiah; Amos). Even in this latter case the full counsel of God is often provided by having another, contemporary prophet preach the opposite pole. In the case of Nahum's audience, the word of judgment upon them had only recently been spoken to them by Micah. Their own sins, therefore, are not at all being ignored. Nahum, however, points out the equity of God's justice. Often here, as in other books, the punishment closely fits the crime. God is not capricious, being taken by sudden whims or fancies, but just (see 1:14, 2:1, 7, *etc.*).

NAHUM

This message of God through Nahum was to encourage God's people. Oppressed by a seemingly invincible foe who had overwhelmed the entire region from the Nile to the Tigris, Israel could not look to her own power, but only to God for deliverance. Yet within a few years, the invincible was no more – vanquished by the hand of God, before whom no nation can stand. The church, also faced with the threats of powers or ideologies, can only stand in the same place as Israel, in reliance on God who is 'great in power' (1:3, NIV).

ANALYSIS

I. TITLE (1:1)
   A. Subject (1:1a)
   B. Form (1:1b)

II. A PSALM TO YAHWEH (1:2–8)
   A. God's character (1:2–3a)
   B. God's power (1:3b–6)
   C. God's character and power realized (1:7–8)

III. GOD'S WRATH PERSONALIZED (1:9–11)

IV. GOD'S DUAL VERDICTS (1:12 – 2:2)
   A. Judah: end of oppression (1:12–13)
   B. Assyria: end of the line (1:14)
   C. Judah: good news (1:15)
   D. Assyria: prepare for battle (2:1)
   E. Judah: ruin restored (2:2)

V. VIGNETTE OF BATTLE (2:3–10)
   A. Attack (2:3–5)
   B. Defeat (2:6–10)

VI. THE LION OF ASSYRIA ROUTED (2:11–13)

VII. WOE TO NINEVEH (3:1–19)
   A. Woe (3:1)
   B. Fighting and death (3:2–3)
   C. The whore's disgrace (3:4–7)
   D. Assyria the invincible? A satire (3:8–17)
      i. Mighty Thebes destroyed (3:8–10)
      ii. Assyrian inadequacy (3:11–13)
      iii. Fruitless preparations (3:14–17)
   E. How the mighty have fallen (3:18–19)

COMMENTARY

I. TITLE (1:1)

A. Subject (1:1a)

The prophecy is in the form of an *oracle* (NIV, JB, RSV; 'burden', AV; see the Introduction, p. 21) or pronouncement, a term usually referring to revelations concerning non-Israelites (*e.g.* Is. 13:1; 15:1, but *cf.* Zc. 12:1; Mal. 1:1; see Je. 23:34–40). Here the subject of the oracle is *Nineveh*, and by extension Assyria, of which it was the capital from the time of Sennacherib (early eighth century BC) until the city's destruction by the Babylonians in 612 BC. Although the literal city is meant here, it could also have symbolic overtones, representing all those who oppose God and his work (see Jonah; Lk. 11:30), as did the Babylonian capital city Babylon at a later period (*cf.* Rev. 18:2, 10, 21).

B. Form (1:1b)

The prophecy's form is that of a document or *book*, most likely in the form of a scroll (Je. 36:2; *cf.* Ezk. 3:1–3) containing a 'revelation' (*cf.* Is. 1:1; Ob. 1) from God, its ultimate source. Being the only prophecy described as a book has led some to suggest that it originally circulated as an underground pamphlet during Assyrian persecution, perhaps during the reign of Manasseh.[1] The prophet is 'Nahum of Elkosh' (RSV), which was most probably his home town. Locations in Assyria, Galilee and Judaea have been identified with Elkosh. The exact location is not certain, although the last suggestion is more likely (see the Introduction, p. 19).

[1] See Rudolph, p. 148; *cf.* Keil, p. 9. Van der Woude, 'Book of Nahum', p. 122, suggests that the prophecy was originally a 'letter' to or from the Israelite exiles.

II. A PSALM TO YAHWEH (1:2–8)

In the form of a descriptive psalm, a hymn describing the being and characteristics of Yahweh (*cf.* Pss. 29; 33; 103; 104; Lk. 1:46–55), God's justifiable wrath against his enemies and against his people's enemies is vividly portrayed. Not being limited by time or space, this opening hymn gives the theological context of the book as showing God's universal power and justice through the example of the nation Assyria.[1] The writer first presents God's character and power in cosmic terms (vv. 2–6) and then on a more personal level (vv. 7–8).

A. God's character (1:2–3a)

2. The personal, covenant God of Israel, 'Yahweh' (JB; *cf.* Ex. 6:2–4), is characterized as being *jealous*, for in his holiness God does not allow rivals (Ex. 20:5; Jos. 24:19; Zc. 8:2). This is a covenant term, indicating that when a relationship between God and his people was entered into, it was to be exclusive of all other parties on both sides (Ex. 6:7; *cf.* Ho. 1:9; 2:23).[2] As a God of justice, he is *avenging* (NIV, RSV) against any injustice (Dt. 32:35; *cf.* Rom. 12:19). Any judgment by God upon sin, whether that of his own people or others, is not based on whim or uncontrollable anger but on God's unchangingly holy character. The correct response to an action, good or bad, will be given by God; neither too little nor too much. Nineveh serves as an example of this characteristic holiness of God, accentuated by the threefold repetition of his avenging acts in one verse. God's jealousy is structurally paralleled[3] to his wrath, the angry reaction of a holy God to sin, whether of pagans or of Israel itself (Rom. 1:18). The target of God's vengeance is *his foes*, against whom he *maintains*

[1] B. S. Childs, *Introduction to the Old Testament as Scripture* (SCM Press/ Fortress, 1979), pp. 443–444.

[2] See J. G. Baldwin, *Haggai, Zechariah, Malachi* (Inter-Varsity Press, 1972), pp. 101–103.

[3] The structure is a chiasm or inverted parallel in the form ABB[1]A[1], *i.e.*:

    A   God is jealous.
    B   Yahweh is an avenger.
    B[1]   Yahweh is an avenger.
    A[1]   [God is] wrathful.

See M. Dahood, 'Chiasmus', *IDBS*, p. 145 and the bibliography there.

[*his wrath*] (though the bracketed object is not in the Heb.; *cf.* Lv. 19:18; Je. 3:5, 12). The verb denotes 'guarding' or 'keeping', suggesting either that God withholds his anger until an appropriate time (see v. 3a), or that he is constantly angry. Another possibility not requiring a missing direct object is to interpret the verb as 'to rage', as it is in Akkadian (*cf.* Am. 1:11; Je. 3:5),[1] with God as one who 'rages' against those who oppose him.

3a. God's 'long-suffering' (Ex. 34:6–7; Nu. 14:18; *cf.* the opposite Heb. idiom in Pr. 14:17) does not negate the previous verse but shows his patience awaiting certain justice. His wait is not unending, since God will not condone sin. Patience coupled with 'great might' (RSV) shows two complementary sides of God's character and is not without parallel in the Old Testament (Nu. 14:17–18; Ne. 9:17).

B. God's power (1:3b–6)

3b–5. God's power in the created order is shown by his close association with some of its mighty manifestations, *whirlwind* and *storm* (*cf.* Ps. 83:15; Is. 29:6), in which he makes his way, stirring up *clouds* with *his feet* as the Israelites stirred the *dust* in their travels. His power is also shown by his ability to reverse creation, drying up the sea and rivers (*cf.* Is. 42:15; 50:2; Je. 51:36; Rev. 21:1) and causing areas of proverbial fruitfulness (*Bashan* in Transjordan, *Carmel* in north Israel, and *Lebanon*; *cf.* Is. 33:9) to *wither* (Is. 16:8; 24:4; 33:9; Joel 1:10, 12). The foundations of the earth itself react to God's powerful presence with earthquake (Ps. 46:3; Je. 4:24) and dissolution (Ps. 46:6; Am. 9:5; *cf.* Am. 9:13 for the verb 'flow' with a positive connotation). The result will be the 'laying waste' (RSV)[2] of the *earth* and all creatures on it, showing God's complete and universal power for building and destroying. As God created from chaos (Gn. 1:2), so he can undo his creation and return it to chaos.

---

[1] See the entry on *nadāru* in E. Reiner, *The Assyrian Dictionary* 11/1 (Oriental Institute, 1980), pp. 59–61; *cf.* Cathcart, pp. 42–43; R. L. Smith, p. 72.

[2] A minor textual emendation, evidenced by the Syr. and Vulg. and adopted by several modern exegetes, involves reading *š* for *ś*, the relocation of one dot by a fraction of an inch, replacing the difficult 'will rise' (*watiśśā'*; AV 'burned') with 'is laid waste' (*watiššā'*; *cf.* Is. 6:11; 17:12–13).

6. God's anger is stressed by using four different Hebrew synonyms, *indignation* (*cf.* Is. 10:5; Je. 10:10), *fierce anger* (a combination of two Hebrew words, each of which separately are used of anger, Ex. 15:7; Ezk. 7:12 and Ex. 32:12; Ne. 9:17) and *wrath* (v. 2; Ps. 59:13 [Heb. v. 14]; Is. 63:5). It is such that none can 'stand before' (AV) it, even brute nature (*cf.* Je. 4:26; Mal. 3:2). The emphatic force is expressed not only by the accumulation of synonyms but also by the use of rhetorical questions (*Who* . . .? *Who* . . .?) forcing the admission: 'No one can stand before God's wrath' (see Additional Note below).

Additional Note on rhetorical questions

Different literary forms or genres serve different functions. That of prophecy is to persuade the hearers to a certain course of action in the light of God's revelation through the prophet. This persuasive function is also that of classical rhetoric, which used certain techniques to achieve its aims. Many of those techniques can also be discerned in Hebrew prophecy, cincluding the use of the rhetorical question.

Unlike a regular question, which is soliciting information, a rhetorical question assumes the answer is already known by both the asker and the asked. Instead of the statement which could have been used in its place, the rhetorical question forces the hearer to get actively involved in the discussion. By his response in supplying the known answer, the hearer himself takes part in the process of persuasion. The technique is used elsewhere in Nahum (2:11; 3:7–8) and in other prophetic texts.[1]

C. God's character and power realized (1:7–8)

In juxtaposition with God's power in wrath, one is again confronted with his patience and grace (*cf.* v. 2). Yahweh's benevolent character is shown towards those seeking him as their protection in times of 'oppression' (*trouble*) rather than relying on their own devices (*cf.* 2 Sa. 22:31, 33; Ps. 37:39–40;

---

[1] For further discussion of the use of rhetoric, including rhetorical questions, in other prophetic texts, see Y. Gitay, *Prophecy and Persuasion: A study of Isaiah 40–48* (Linguistica Biblica, 1981).

contrast Dt. 32:37; Is. 30:1–3).[1] In contrast, God's enemies will experience *darkness*[2] and *flood*, bringing to *an end* 'its place', apparently referring to Nineveh (*cf.* v. 1; so NIV).[3]

III. GOD'S WRATH PERSONALIZED (1:9–11)

9. The style now changes. The writer addresses Assyria directly as 'you' (see RSV; the Heb. verb is in the second person plural). *Whatever* Assyria 'plots' (RSV; *cf.* Dn. 11:24; Ho. 7:15) in opposition to Yahweh will come to nothing as a result of God's actions (see v. 8). So complete is this end that Assyria will not be troubled again, nor will she cause further trouble, because she will be no more.

10. Difficulties in text and syntax make this verse one of the most difficult to interpret in the Old Testament. The verse provides the detail of Assyria's destruction noted in verse 9, and the ground or basis for the statement of God's intervention in that verse,[4] which is known 'because' of what will be observed. The particle used could alternatively be understood

[1] Some see the first two Heb. words in v. 8 completing v. 7, 'Those who take refuge in him in an overwhelming flood' (Cathcart, p. 31; Rudolph, p. 152), but the copula 'and' at the start of v. 8 does not make this proposal syntactically likely.

[2] The syntax allows either the possibility that God is the subject, with 'darkness' being the accusative of place or direction (G-K 118, d-g; *cf.* Cathcart, p. 31), or that 'darkness' is the grammatical subject (LXX, Vulg., Syr.).

[3] Some commentators, seeing the reference to Nineveh in 1:1 as a secondary addition, and thus being left with a referential pronoun without an antecedent in 1:8 (*i.e.* 'make an end of *it*', where NIV supplies 'Nineveh'), arbitrarily propose that the object of the verb is 'his adversaries', an emendation of *mᵉqômâh* to *bᵉqamaw*; *cf.* Ps. 59:1; see *e.g.* LXX; *BHS*; Cathcart. D. T. Tsumura, 'Janus Parallelism in Nah 1:8', *JBL* 102 (1983), pp. 109–111, has shown that the meaning of 'rebel' can be derived without altering the present consonantal text, reading it *mᵉqawmâ*. He suggests that the consonants *m* in the word above, and *b* 'in', both labials, sound similar enough to allow a word play on two possible meanings of the word, 'its place' connecting the line using synthetic parallelism with v. 8a, and '(in) the rebel(s)', synonymously parallel to the 'foes' in v. 8c. It is also the case in some instances that the Heb. 'place' means 'the place of God's enemies', with the opposition or oppression implied (*cf.* Ps. 37:10).

[4] The NEB, RSV and JB (*cf. BHS* note) read the opening Heb. particle *kî* as *kᵉ*, 'like', 'as', even though the existing form does have a causal use which fits the context without emendation (see Gn. 3:14; Is. 28:15). The NIV ignores the word and that which follows.

as emphasizing the certainty of the condition in this verse, 'certainly',[1] though this rare usage would be less likely. The degree or measure of God's punishment is expressed as Assyria going 'as far as'[2] being *entangled* (*cf.* Gn. 22:13; Is. 9:18) like *thorns*, which are elsewhere vulnerable to destruction by fire (Ec. 7:6; *cf.* Jdg. 9:15; Is. 9:18; 10:17 and elsewhere, where different Heb. words for 'thorn' are used). Assyria is unable to free herself from God's fiery judgment. She will be destroyed or consumed (Ex. 3:2) 'completely',[3] as fire devours *dry stubble*, which is known not only for its inflammability (Ex. 15:7; Is. 5:24; Ob. 18) but also for its uselessness (Jb. 13:25), as are thorns (Jdg. 9:15). The inability to act usefully in the face of God's wrath is accentuated with another metaphor, comparing them to 'sodden drunkards' (*cf.* Pr. 23:20).[4] The inebriation could have resulted from Assyria's deep draughts from the cup of God's wrath (*cf.* Je. 25:27; 51:57). The two metaphors of fire and drunkenness are mixed, and the syntax makes the exact nature of the comparison unclear, resulting in variations between different translations,[5] but what is clearly portrayed is the certainty of God's punishment.

11. Assyria is accused of giving rise to *one . . . who plots evil against the Lord* (see v. 9), either referring generally to all Assyrian kings, or more specifically to Sennacherib who mounted an invasion of Judah in 701 BC (2 Ki. 18:13 – 19:36). This same person also *counsels wickedness* or, reading the second word as a proper name, advises Belial, a demon or even Satan himself (*cf.* v. 15; 2 Cor. 6:15; 11QMelch; 1QS 1:18, 24 and *passim*). The specific reason for the destruction of Assyria, in keeping with God's judicial character (vv. 2–6), is thus the wicked attack on God and his people rather than any national chauvinism on the part of Israel.

---

[1] For the asseverative use, see G-K para. 149; R. J. Williams, *Hebrew Syntax: An Outline* (University of Toronto, 1967), p. 74.

[2] *'ad*, see *BDB*, p. 724.

[3] The adverb can grammatically qualify the dryness as being complete.

[4] Lit. 'and drunken men when they drink', grammatically being very problematic, with the proposed reading being only tentative.

[5] The Hebrew *'ad* has been ignored or revocalized, though the context seems to demand a comparison (so RSV, NEB, JB), which is one of the uses of the word (*cf.* 2 Sa. 23:19; 1 Ch. 4:27), although not with exactly the nuance required here.

IV. GOD'S DUAL VERDICTS (1:12 – 2:2)

In the form of an oracle (v. 12, *This is what the Lord says*) to two parties in a legal dispute, God pronounces his verdicts alternately to Judah, for her acquittal and hope (vv. 12–13, 15; 2:2), and to Assyria, for her destruction (v. 14; 2:1).

A. Judah: end of oppression (1:12–13)

The first message to Judah is that of hope; her enemies will be confounded and she will find relief. The exact reading is difficult,[1] but the idea conveyed is that neither numbers nor strength will win the day for Assyria. Their burdensome tyranny (*yoke*, *cf.* Je. 28:10–14; Ezk. 30:18; *shackles*, *cf.* Je. 2:20; 30:8) will be removed and Assyria will be gone. From Judah's point of view, she will find relief from her earlier oppression.

B. Assyria: end of the line (1:14)

At Yahweh's command, Assyria will reach its end due to a lack of *descendants*[2] (*cf.* 1 Sa. 24:21; Is. 14:20–22), and will be buried, like a despised and worthless thing to be disposed of (*cf.* Gn. 16:4–6). As it was the Assyrian practice to desecrate conquered shrines (2 Ki. 18:33–35; *cf.* 25:9; 2 Ch. 36:7; Ezr. 1:7), so their temples and idols will be destroyed.

C. Judah: good news (1:15)[3]

In a statement strongly resembling the Messianic passage in Isaiah 52:7 (*cf.* Is. 40:9), Judah's attention is directed to the news of *peace* and well-being proclaimed by a 'herald' (Gk., 'evangelist') as one who brings welcome *news*. This news arises from the downfall of her oppressor, designated as 'Belial', or *the wicked* (*cf.* v. 11). Assyria is to be 'cut off' *completely*, no longer to be a threat. Instead of terror, Judah will now be

---

[1] The LXX divides the consonantal text of v. 12 differently and misses out four letters when it reads 'one who rules much water' instead of 'though they be strong and many' (RSV; *cf.* Syr., *BHS*).

[2] The proposed emendation of *BHS* to 'your name will not be remembered' is gratuitous and unnecessary.

[3] This verse is numbered 2:1 in the Hebrew text, reflecting the lack of chapter and verse divisions until the twelfth century AD.

able to fulfil her religious obligations in the form of the *festivals* which were commanded of her (*cf.* Nu. 28 – 29) and her sacred *vows* (*cf.* Nu. 30; Dt. 23:21–23).

D. Assyria: prepare for battle (2:1)

Assyria, herself the perennial aggressor, is now faced with attack by a 'scatterer',[1] a military coalition of Medes and Babylonians (see the Introduction, p. 20). She is satirically called to prepare herself by setting guards on the fortresses and roads (3:14; Je. 46:3–6). No amount of preparation, however, will enable her to withstand the onslaught, since it is God who is her opponent. This motif of battle preparation, ending the verdicts directed towards Assyria, binds this section to the following vivid battle scene (2:3–10), where it is picked up and developed.

E. Judah: ruin restored (2:2)

Yahweh's restoration of 'Judah's (MT 'Jacob's') *splendour*[2] is hoped to parallel that of Israel in the north. A rebuilding of the entire people of God is desired, since they had been completely 'plundered' (*cf.* Is. 24:1,3) by Assyria and Babylonia. Thus, even after the fall of the northern kingdom, a complete restoration of the nation is desired (*cf.* Ezk. 37:15–23; Zc. 10:6–12) though not yet actualized in the form of a restored and unified nation. The New Testament interprets a similar passage in Amos 9:11–12 to indicate the inclusion of the Gentiles within the people of God as being its fulfilment (Acts 15:13–19), so also the present passage could see its fruition in the church as the reunited nation of Israel (*cf.* Jas. 1:1).

---

[1] The subject of the sentence is variously understood as a 'scatterer' or 'router' of armies (*cf.* 2 Sa. 22:15; Ps. 18:14; Is. 24:1) or as a 'shatterer' (*cf.* RSV; Je. 51:20), depending on whether one reads the word as *mēpîts* (MT) or *mēpēts*.

[2] Some substitute 'vine' for splendour' (*cf.* 'branches' later in the verse), but without textual support, and it is not necessary since Heb. poetry commonly used repetition.

V. VIGNETTE OF BATTLE (2:3–10)

The judgment of Nineveh and Assyria is expressed in clear, military terms. The vividness of this battle description has led some to propose a post-612 BC date for at least this portion of the prophecy (see the Introduction, p. 20). Such a conclusion is not compelling. Armies and war were part of Israel's experience throughout most of her history, thus placing the imagery readily to hand.

A. Attack (2:3–5)

3–4. The motif of battle is picked up from verse 1 with increased detail. The visual imagery of colourful uniform and flashing weapon is augmented by the sound of clattering wheel and careering chariot. Some read *the metal on the chariots* (v. 3) as 'torches' (AV, RSV; *cf.* v. 4), arising from a transposition of two Hebrew letters, though the textual evidence for the present reading is strong. The *pine* ('fir', AV) which is *brandished* is more probably spears or other weaponry made from this wood (so NIV) rather than the trees themselves (as AV).

5. The soldiers, mustered by their leader, *stumble* in their haste to reach the wall, where they set up a *protective shield* ('mantelet', RSV), a portable cover to protect the besiegers from objects hurled from the walls under attack. Some interpret this as a reference to the defending forces (*e.g.* AV), but the grammatical reference to the musterer (*he summons*, NIV) appears best to have as its antecedent the 'scatterer' of verse 1.[1]

B. Defeat (2:6–10)

The actual downfall of Nineveh is referred to only briefly (v. 6), while its results are detailed more fully (vv. 7–10).

6. The identification of the *river gates* is uncertain. Probably they were part of the canal and channel system directing water through the city. It has been suggested that a contributing factor to the city's defeat was a flood, causing, among other things, the *palace* to 'melt' from the water,[2] although there is

---

[1] The RSV, following the LXX, revocalizes the first verb of the verse, reading it as a plural passive, *i.e.* 'The officers are summoned'.
[2] See Wiseman, *IBD*, p. 1090.

no supporting extra-biblical documentation of this proposal since the Babylonian Chronicle concerning the fall of Nineveh is broken at this point.[1] The verb 'melt' is also used metaphorically of 'dismay' (*e.g.* Is. 14:31; Ezk. 21:15; *cf.* RSV).

7. *It is* 'established' (Gn. 28:12; *cf. decreed* NIV),[2] determined by God, that the captive Nineveh should be *exiled*, suffering the same fate Assyria had previously laid upon those whom she had conquered, including Israel (*cf.* 2 Ki. 17). Assyria's defeat is accentuated in that even 'her maids' *moan* and *beat upon their breasts*, showing their anguish.

8–9. Now the subject of this graphic description is shown by name to be *Nineveh*. In a metaphor her troops are likened to a *pool* (of water) as used in irrigation (Ec. 2:6), but whose waters[3] escape, rendering it useless. The rout of the Assyrian forces is not even stopped by a cry to 'wait'. All flee, *no-one turns back*. As a result, Nineveh's enemies can now *plunder* and despoil the once proud city. Her riches are boundless because she herself had in the past been one who plundered others.

10. The terror of stricken Nineveh is graphically described using physiological manifestations of fear. A three-part Hebrew word play further serves to emphasize her 'desolation' and 'ruin' (RSV).[4]

VI. THE LION OF ASSYRIA ROUTED (2:11–13)

The writer changes from describing an anticipated battle to a metaphor in which the Assyrian lion, which was formerly ferocious, has been driven away.

11–12. A taunt in the form of a rhetorical question (*cf.* 1:6; 3:7–8, and see the Additional Note on rhetorical questions,

[1] *ANET*, pp. 304–305.

[2] The interpretation of *ḥuṣṣab* is debated. In addition to the proposal given here (*cf.* J. M. P. Smith, p. 331), it is seen as a proper name 'Huzzab', as yet unattested elsewhere (*e.g.* Maier, pp. 256, 261), or as corrupt, and so amended, although without textual support.

[3] The awkward Heb. form has been read 'all her days' (Keil, p. 25; *cf.* Maier, p. 263), following the present punctuation (*mîmê hî'*), or 'its water', following the LXX and requiring textual emendation (*mêmeyhā*; BHS).

[4] The progressive stages of intensifying dereliction are indicated by three Hebrew words, each adding one syllable to the preceding word, *i.e. bûqâ, mᵉbûqâ, mᵉbullāqâ*.

p. 29) is asked concerning the dwelling and feeding place[1] where the lion had previously stalked unopposed. Here the pride had killed its prey and adequately provided for its sustenance.

13. Yahweh's opposition to Nineveh is declared in an oracle (*cf.* the stark contrast in Rom. 8:31). The metaphor is mixed between the lions, whose 'cubs' are destroyed and whose *prey* is 'cut off' (RSV), and the earlier battle scene (vv. 3–10) of the burning of chariotry and the silencing of the military *messengers* in the destruction. This verse thus structurally unites the chapter and brings it to a conclusion.

VII. WOE TO NINEVEH (3:1–19)

The downfall of Nineveh is pictured from several different points in time: looking ahead towards opposition (vv. 5–12), preparing for siege and battle (vv. 14–17), participating in an actual battle (vv. 2–4) and looking back on defeat (vv. 13, 18–19).

A. Woe (3:1)

Woe, as an interjection used in lamenting the dead (1 Ki. 13:30; Je. 34:5; *cf.* Am. 5:16), is used with an extended meaning in the prophetic literature to introduce a dire threat (Is. 5; Hab. 2). Its force is that the punishment threatened is so certain that those addressed are as good as dead. This is accentuated in Hebrew by the lament or *qînâ* metrical pattern (3+2) in the first half of the verse. The use of the form here is ironic, since the demise of the tyrant would be welcomed, not mourned. The 'bloody city' (RSV), Nineveh, is lamented. She who was the place of *lies* (Ho. 7:3), *plunder* and 'prey' (the latter a recollection of the oracle in 2:11–13) will now find her position reversed, receiving the destruction she had previously dispensed.

---

[1] So the AV, NIV and several commentators. With one letter transposed, resulting in 'cave', see the RSV and other commentators.

B. Fighting and death (3:2–3)

The vividness of battle is resumed from 2:3–10 with the sights and sounds of attackers on the move (v. 2), and with the inevitable aftermath of war, numberless *corpses* (v. 3).

C. The whore's disgrace (3:4–7)

The cause of Assyria's downfall is given in the form of another metaphor, that of a prostitute (*cf.* Is. 23:16; Ezk. 16; 23; Rev. 17–18) who, having degraded others, will now be repaid by her own degradation.

4. Not only does Assyria's unrestrained fornication contribute to her ruin, so also do her *sorceries* (*cf.* 2 Ki. 9:22; 2 Ch. 33:6; Mi. 5:12), the arcane arts undertaken to determine the divine will (*cf.* Is. 47:9, 12–13). She used both to subjugate other nations, and they will now contribute to her own judgment.

5–6. In another oracular confrontation, driving home the certainty of God's judgment by using the same words as started the oracle in 2:13, Yahweh turns the tables on Assyria. Because she, like a prostitute, had eagerly exposed her *nakedness* as part of her trade, so too it will be exposed to her shame before the surrounding *nations* (*cf.* Is. 47:3; Je. 13:22, 26; Ezk. 16:37–39; Ho. 2:3, 9). They will show their disgust as they *pelt* the whore with *filth* (Mal. 2:3; *cf.* 2 Ki. 10:27) and make her *a spectacle* for the contempt of passers-by, matching the use of stocks and pillory in the more recent past.

7. The revulsion of the 'spectators' (*rō'ayik*, a word play on 'spectacle', *kᵉrō'îy*, in v. 6) leads to turning away in abhorrence. One is rhetorically asked if any will mourn. The answer, as is often the case for such questions (*cf.* 1:6; 2:11; 3:8, and the Additional Note on rhetorical questions, p. 29), is negative – 'no-one': no-one to *mourn* and no-one to *comfort*. She who had been merciless will receive no mercy.

D. Assyria the invincible? A satire (3:8–17)

The precedent of another capital whose strength did not save her from destruction (Egyptian Thebes) is presented as a goad to prick the already demoralized Assyrian capital. In comparison to Thebes, Nineveh is feeble. The scene is now

moved back in time to a point prior to the actual assault (*cf.*
2:3–10; 3:2–3), for which preparation is still to be made.

i. Mighty Thebes destroyed (3:8–10). 8–9. *Thebes* (Heb.,
nō' 'āmôn), in spite of its natural water defences[1] and military
alliances with Ethiopia (*Cush*; *cf.* Zp. 2:12), *Put* (Gn. 10:6) and
Libya (2 Ch. 12:3), was brought to nought (see Is. 11:11; 19 –
20 and the Introduction, p. 20). Nineveh is rhetorically asked
if she considers herself Thebes' equal, and again the answer
must be 'no' (*cf.* 1:6; 2:11; 3:7).

10. Thebes' ultimate end is described in terms reminiscent
of the degradation inflicted by Mesopotamians on others: *exile*
(2 Ki. 17:6; 18:11; 24:15); captivity (2 Ch. 30:9 [*cf.* 2
Ch. 30:6b]; Is. 20:4; Je. 41:10; Ob. 11); slaughter of infants
(Ho. 10:14; 13:16; *cf.* 2 Ki. 8:12; Ps. 137:9; Is. 13:16); *lots . . .
cast for . . . nobles*, to determine where they should be exiled
(Joel 3:3; Ob. 11); and *chains* (*cf.* 2 Ki. 25:7; Ps. 149:8;
Je. 40:1,4). The fate of Thebes would lead Assyria to expect
that her punishment might follow the same lines.

ii. Assyrian inadequacy (3:11–13). The parallel between
Nineveh and Thebes (vv. 8–10) is made explicit when
Nineveh is told that she will suffer a similar fate.

11. A linguistic parallel with the description of Thebes' fate
is the particle 'also/yet' (*gam*), found twice in verse 10 and
echoed twice in this verse. Assyria's state will be that of
staggering inebriation from the wine of God's wrath
(Je. 25:15–17; Ob. 16; Hab. 2:16), and a cowering fear of the
enemy.

12. The vulnerable state of Assyria is well illustrated by the
metaphor of fruit so ripe for plucking that it falls into the open
mouths of those who shake the tree. This could be another
echo of the picture of the voracious Assyrian lion (2:12).

13. Scorn is poured on the might of Assyria. This might
was based on *troops*,[2] who in strength and ferocity are like

---

[1] Situated among the Nile channels, water played an important part in
Theban life. The city lies considerably inland, so a reference to the sea as
part of its defences would itself be inaccurate were it not for the Hebrew *yām*
applying elsewhere to major rivers, the Nile (*e.g.* Is. 18:1–2; Ezk. 32:2) and
the Euphrates (Je. 51:36).

[2] Hebrew *'am* refers firstly to 'people' in general, but also, on a more
restricted level, to 'troops' (Nu. 20:20; 21:23).

women, the weaker sex (*cf.* Is. 19:16; Je. 50:37; 51:30). It is also founded on the false protection of *open gates* for the towns, with their ruined cross-bars (*cf.* Dt. 3:5; Jdg. 16:3). None of these are able to carry out their defensive function. Security is gone.

iii. Fruitless preparations (3:14–17). 14–16. Assyria is ironically commanded to lay in supplies and *strengthen* her fortifications in preparation for a siege, even though *fire* (*cf.* Is. 1:7; Je. 49:27; Am. 7:4) and *sword* (*cf.* Jb. 1:15–17; Ezk. 38:21–22) will destroy her. The totality of destruction is compared to that by the grasshopper (see Ps. 78:46; Joel 1:4), which sweeps away all in its path. Assyria is reminded of her *merchants* (Ezk. 17:4; 27; Rev. 18:11–20), who had multiplied greatly, as is known from the historical records from as far away as Cappadocia in Asia Minor.[1] These merchants are portrayed negatively, comparing in rapacity and transience to the locust swarm.

17. The last mentioned characteristic of the locust, its fleeting presence, is also used to describe Assyria's *guards* and *officials*[2] who disappear at the slightest excuse. Thus the economic (v. 16) and military (v. 17) bureaucracy upon which Assyria depended does not provide the expected support, but rather itself leads in the panicked flight from the invaders.

E. How the mighty have fallen (3:18–19)

In a closing address directly to the Assyrian monarch, the complete lack of support for leader and population shows the irreparability of the nation's position.

18. The king is told that his *shepherds*, those invested with responsibility for the direction and rule of the people (Je. 17:16; Zc. 10:2–3), and his *nobles* are sleeping on the job. They will provide no help in the coming invasion. Neither will the general population who have dispersed. Restoring the *scattered* people should be the duty of the shepherds, but they are not fulfilling it.

19. Assyria the mighty is dying from an incurable *wound*.

---

[1] See J. D. Hawkins (ed.), *Trade in the Ancient Near East* (British School of Archaeology in Iraq, 1977); E. Lipinski, *State and Temple Economy in the Ancient Near East* (Leuven University, 1979).

[2] From the Akkadian word for 'scribe' as a class of official at times involved in military conscription duties; *cf.* Je. 51:27.

Due to her own *endless cruelty* and exploitation of others, this extremity is viewed not with compassion but with joy, as those who hear of it exult with clapping *hands* (*cf.* Pss. 47:1; 98:8; Is. 55:12; Ezk. 25:6). Foremost among those rejoicing would be Judah, for whose encouragement and support the prophecy is given. Rejoicing is not in this context gleeful gloating at the misfortune of others (*cf.* Ps. 22:17; Ob. 12; Rev. 11:10), an attitude which is unacceptable for the people of God. Rather, it is pleasure at the vindication of God and his promises. His justice and holiness are upheld because, not only is he gracious to bless those who turn to him in repentance, he is also righteous in his dealings with sin and rebellion against himself and his people (*cf.* Rev. 11:16–18; 15:3–4; 16:4–7). One's response as an individual or as a nation to God and his will, whether in acceptance or rejection, thus has major implications for blessing or judgment.

HABAKKUK

INTRODUCTION

I. THE MAN

HABAKKUK loved God, but he was prepared, as few others would be, to engage him in a probing dialogue about the rightness of his actions. Most believers, of course, encounter a time in their spiritual life when they doubt or question God. Few, however, as Job did, openly debate the issues. Even rarer is an individual who will stand before God and confront him with apparent anomalies in his actions towards mankind. This is what the prophet Habakkuk did, even going a step beyond this to challenging God on the response which he gives to Habakkuk's initial question.

One of the roles of a prophet was to serve as an intermediary between the God of Israel and his people. He was to indicate when they strayed from the covenant into which they had voluntarily entered, and urge them to return to it. Habakkuk takes it upon himself to work in the other direction, calling God to account when his actions did not seem to correspond to those demanded by the covenant. The situation of a prophet was precarious enough when he confronted his people, but it is a very rare individual who will put himself completely on the line by confronting his God. Such a man was Habakkuk.

Less is stated in the Bible concerning Habakkuk than almost any other prophet. Not even his father, tribe or hometown are mentioned. His name is apparently not Hebrew but comes from the Akkadian word for some plant or fruit tree.[1] Akkadian speakers were intimately involved in the life of Israel at this period (see p. 44 below).

Later tradition sought to identify Habakkuk more closely. The apocryphal 'Daniel, Bel, and the Snake' has Habakkuk bringing food to Daniel to sustain him during his week in the

---

[1] See the entry on *habbaququ* in A. L. Oppenheim, *The Assyrian Dictionary*, 6 (Oriental Institute, 1956), p. 13.

lion's den. One manuscript describes him as a son of Jesus, a Levite. This note, along with the association of Habakkuk with music, especially the psalm in chapter 3 (see vv. 1, 19), an aspect of the cult especially associated with Levites (Ezr. 3:10; Ne. 12:27), and his title as 'the prophet' (1:1), has suggested to some that he was a professional temple prophet, though the existence of such a functionary is not proven.[1]

II. THE TIMES

The time periods during which Habakkuk prophesied and during which the book was written have been a matter of debate.[2] From 1:6, it appears that an invasion of the Babylonians, or 'Chaldeans' as they were referred to by the biblical writers,[3] is in the offing. The Neo-Babylonian Empire gained power under Nabopolassar from about 625 BC, gaining strength in 612 BC with the destruction of the Assyrian capital, Nineveh, and reaching a peak in 605 BC with the defeat of Egypt and her allies at Carchemish in Syria by Nebuchadnezzar (Je. 46:2).[4] The invasion anticipated by Habakkuk could have been any time prior to 587 BC, when Jerusalem was finally destroyed by the Babylonians. These prophecies were probably given some time earlier. A suitable period is the reign of Jehoiakim (609–598 BC), for it was during his reign that the Babylonian presence was increasingly felt.[5] They marched against Judah in 598 BC, and Jehoiakim then died, possibly by assassination (*cf.* Je. 22:18–19; 36:30). The personal knowledge of the Babylonian brutality (*cf.* 1:12–17) accords well with this period. Habakkuk was thus a contemporary of Nahum, Zephaniah and Jeremiah.

Judah had witnessed the downfall and exile of her northern sister Israel slightly more than a century previously. She herself had not learnt, however, that repeated violation of the covenant with God on her own part would not be left unpunished forever. She would now, according to the pro-

---

[1] See J. A. Motyer, 'Prophecy, Prophets', *IBD*, p. 1283.
[2] See Jöcken, pp. 3–106, for a discussion of the various options proposed.
[3] See D. J. Wiseman, 'Chaldea, Chaldeans', *IBD*, pp. 257–258 and W. G. Lambert, 'The Babylonians and Chaldeans', *POTT*, pp. 179–196.
[4] See A. K. Grayson, *Assyrian and Babylonian Chronicles* (J. J. Augustin, 1975), p. 99.
[5] See J. Bright, *A History of Israel* (SCM Press/Westminster, ³1980), p. 333.

phet, be faced with a similar fate herself.

The prophecy anticipates the Babylonian's defeat, which finally took place before the combined power of the Indo-Aryan Medes and Persians who, under Cyrus, captured Babylon in 539 BC.

III. THE BOOK

Habakkuk stands eighth among the Minor Prophets, between Nahum and Zephaniah, who were roughly contemporary in time and shared a view of Yahweh's justice, sovereignty and grace.

The structure of the book is straightforward, with two questions put to God by Habakkuk, each of which is followed by God's response. The first concerns Yahweh's apparent toleration of sin, especially injustice (1:2–4), and is followed by the assurance that it will be dealt with by God using the Chaldean or Neo-Babylonian Empire as his instrument (1:5–11). This first answer thus appears to be directed towards the Babylonian destruction of Jerusalem in 587 BC (see p. 44). But this raises a yet greater moral problem for Habakkuk. How can he use as instruments of judgment a people who are much more cruel and inhumane than those who are being punished (1:12–17)? Habakkuk expectantly awaits a response (2:1), which comes when Yahweh promises judgment for Babylonia (2:2–20). God's second answer thus relates to the conquest of Babylonia by the Persians in 539 BC (see above). Habakkuk responds to this assurance of God's justice and love in a psalm of worship (ch. 3), which recalls God's coming to meet Israel at Sinai (3:3–7) and his acting as a mighty warrior on her behalf (3:8–15). The book closes with a moving expression of the prophet's trust in his God (3:16–19a).

Two major problems of interpretation arise from a study of the book. The first involves the identity of the wicked whose continued existence without punishment so perplexes Habakkuk (1:4). Who are they, and how do they relate to the wicked of 1:13? Also, who are the righteous in each of these verses? A range of proposals has been put forward, depending, among other things, on the date proposed for the book. Suggestions include the Assyrians, Egyptians, Chaldeans, Greeks, Seleucids, or portions of Judah itself. Within the latter group have been proposed some specific factions,[1] but not enough evidence is available to allow us to be that specific. The wicked in 1:4 are most probably a portion of the Judaean people who, in turning their backs on Yahwism and the law of Moses, are causing grief to those who still follow God's ways. God's judgment upon them will take the form of invasion by the Babylonian armies, which Habakkuk finds intolerable, since in comparison to the ruthless Babylonians even the wicked of Judah are 'more righteous' (1:13) than they.

The wicked in 1:4 and 1:13 must refer to two different groups, because if the wicked of the former verse were either the Assyrians or the Egyptians, who both at times plagued Judah,[2] then the righteous would have to be Judah as a whole. However, though one could then see why Habakkuk would call upon Yahweh to punish the foreign oppressor and free his people, his reaction to God's response would not be understandable, for he would not have had any moral difficulty over any amount of punishment inflicted on pagan oppressors. The prophet's reaction makes sense only if the wicked of 1:4 are a group within Judah and the wicked of 1:13 are the Babylonian invaders sent by God to punish them. It follows that the righteous of 1:4 are those within Judah who experience and grieve over injustice and oppression, whereas in 1:13 the righteous are Judah considered as a whole, in contrast to the much more evil Babylonians.

The second problem involves the place of chapter 3 within the book. The Qumran material includes a commentary on the first two chapters of the book, but not the third.[3] On the basis of the lack of the psalm there, it has been suggested that it is a secondary addition to the book. One problem with this suggestion involves when it might have been added, since it is in all the LXX manuscripts and has been found in a number of texts from the third and second centuries BC.[4] Its non-appearance at Qumran is more likely explained by its lesser

---

[1] See E. Nielsen, 'The Righteous and the Wicked in Habaqquq', *Studia Theologica* 6 (1953), pp. 54–78; M. D. Johnson, 'The Paralysis of the Torah in Habakkuk i4', *VT* 35 (1985), pp. 257–266.

[2] See Bright, *History of Israel*, pp. 310–331.

[3] See Brownlee.

[4] See Brownlee, and J. T. Milik, *Ten Years of Discovery in the Wilderness of Judah* (A. R. Allenson, 1957), pp. 14, 18.

relevance to the needs and interests of the community than the material from the first two chapters. Its non-inclusion does not prove its non-existence any more than the omission of many Old Testament passages and books from current preaching proves that they have dropped out of the canon of Scripture.

IV. THE MESSAGE

The role of a prophet was to bring the nation and its leaders back to obedience to the covenant which God had made with his people at Sinai. If covenant obligations were neglected or abandoned, the prophet, often at some personal peril, would confront the wrongdoers and demand repentance in the name of Yahweh. In the case of Habakkuk, and with even greater personal risk, the prophet confronts Yahweh himself. In this case it is not a call for help for the nation, as is found elsewhere (*cf.* Pss. 10; 12; 44; 60; 74), but a call for judgment upon those who sin (1:2–4). These wicked ones have been variously identified (see pp. 45–46), but apparently are Judaeans who have abandoned God's laws. As Israel cannot with impunity break her covenant, neither may Yahweh allow his covenant to be broken without reacting. Because God seems to be acting against his just and righteous character by not taking action (v. 2), he is brought to task by the prophet. This questioning of God as to whether he is indeed in control of the world is similar to that of Job. He too was faced by a situation where his 'systematic theology' of God did not correspond to his actual experience of God's ways (*cf.* Jb. 6:28–30; 7:11, 20–21; 9:21, *etc.*; see also Je. 12).

Unlike Job, Habakkuk is given a direct answer (1:5–11): punishment will come, but through the instrumentality of the Babylonians. This raises yet further theological and moral problems for the prophet, since the 'cure' of a Babylonian invasion is worse than the 'illness' of Judaean sin. The Babylonians were pagans and not worshippers of Yahweh at all, so how could God use them to punish his own people? Also their cruelty was proverbial and the punishment seemed to be greater than the crime could warrant (1:12–17).

God answers by saying that his chosen instrument for Judah's discipline is itself morally responsible for its actions and will not go without suitable punishment (2:2–20). Not

47

only is this presented in a negative way, picturing judgment and death for the wrongdoer, but also in a positive message of life. In one of the Old Testament statements which has had a profound influence on the history of the church, Judah is told that wrongdoers will be punished for their deeds, but that 'the just shall live by his faith' (2:4, AV). If Judah, or any of God's covenant people, abides by the stipulations of God's covenant, whether old or new, the One in whom they believe and whom they serve will see that they will live. Habakkuk responds to this promise of hope and judgment with a prayer of reverence and faith (ch. 3). He recalls Yahweh's approach to his people at Sinai (vv. 3–7) and his power as the mighty warrior (vv. 8–15). In the light of these evidences of God's being and power in the past, Habakkuk puts himself, in fearful but joyful submission, into the hands and care of the One who can and does provide even when all other means of support and sustenance fail (vv. 16–19).

ANALYSIS

I. TITLE (1:1)

II. THE PROBLEM OF UNPUNISHED WICKEDNESS (1:2–4)

III. YAHWEH'S FIRST RESPONSE (1:5–11)

IV. THE PROBLEM OF EXCESSIVE PUNISHMENT (1:12–17)

V. AWAITING AN ANSWER (2:1)

VI. YAHWEH'S SECOND RESPONSE (2:2–20)
    A. A vision (2:2–5)
        i. Announcement (2:2–3)
        ii. Life and death (2:4–5)
    B. Taunting woes (2:6–20)
        i. The pillager (2:6–8)
        ii. The plotter (2:9–11)
        iii. The promoter of violence (2:12–14)
        iv. The debaucher (2:15–17)
        v. The pagan idolator (2:18–20)

VII. HABAKKUK'S PSALM (3:1–19)
    A. Musical notes (3:1, 19b)
    B. Petition (3:2)
    C. God's powerful presence in history (3:3–15)
        i. God's coming (3:3–7)
        ii. God's combat (3:8–15)
    D. Fear and faith (3:16–19a)

COMMENTARY

I. TITLE (1:1)

The *oracle* (see p. 21) was *received* 'in a vision' (NEB, JB) by *Habakkuk*, who is here called a *prophet*. This title is rare in book headings (see Hg. 1:1; Zc. 1:1), and is taken by some to indicate that Habakkuk was a professional prophet, one who earned his living serving as a prophet at the Temple or court, unlike Amos (*cf.* Am. 7:14). While this is not certain, he at least was recognized in this period of apostasy as one who spoke the message of God.

II. THE PROBLEM OF UNPUNISHED WICKEDNESS (1:2–4)

This section is in the form of a lament, or psalm of complaint, where a need is described and help is sought from God (*cf.* Pss. 3; 13; 22; *etc.*). God's justice is in doubt because his judgment is long delayed.

2. *How long* is a lament introduction (*cf.* Ps. 13:1–2), which shows that the prophet is not afraid to question Yahweh, his God (*cf.* Is. 6:11; see p. 43). Such anguished questions are especially relevant when cries to God are apparently not heard or answered (*cf.* Ps. 22:1). Here the problem is expressed in the cry for aid, as *violence*, continued oppression (*cf.* Gn. 6:11; Jdg. 9:24; and six times in Habakkuk), causes the author to doubt God's ability or desire to intervene or save (*cf.* Dt. 20:4; Pss. 18:41; 33:16–19; Is. 59:1–2; Je. 42:11). The prophet's theological understanding of God as just and righteous is not matched by his experience of God, a problem similar to that known by Job (see Jb. 6:28–30).

3. The severity of the oppression is indicated by piling up synonyms of *injustice* (NIV, JB; *cf.* Pr. 19:28; Is. 29:20; 59:4,

6–7), 'trouble' (RSV; *wrong*, NIV; *cf.* Nu. 23:21; Pr. 24:2; Is. 10:1), *destruction* (*cf.* Is. 22:4; Hab. 2:17), *violence* (v. 2; 2:17), *strife* (*cf.* Pr. 17:1; Je. 15:10) and *conflict* (*cf.* Pr. 15:18; 16:28). *Why*, Habakkuk asks – a typical lament question (see v. 2; *cf.* 1:13; Ps. 22:1; Je. 20:18) – are all these things present in the prophet's life?

4. These continued injustices result in *the law* (the major force which should hold them in check) being *paralysed*.[1] The law was to be the basis of God's order for society (*cf.* Ex. 18:16, 20; Is. 2:3; Je. 32:23), but it no longer functions in this way. The result is an absence of *justice* (*cf.* Is. 1:17; Mi. 6:8), or rather its perversion (RSV, NEB, NIV). In consequence the righteous in Israel are being mistreated by *the wicked*, who *hem* them in. The identity of the latter is one of the debated issues of the book (see the Introduction, pp. 45–46). Here they appear to be the ungodly, unruly people within Israel itself (contrast 1:13). This highlights the reverse aspect of Habakkuk's problem. Not only does injustice go unchecked (v. 2), but the forces of righteousness are thwarted.

III. YAHWEH'S FIRST RESPONSE (1:5–11)

Yahweh answers Habakkuk in an oracle. The speaker is not explicitly identified in a heading or in a concluding statement, but Yahweh is speaking in the first person. The hoped-for response to a lament (*cf.* 1:2–4) would be an oracle of salvation, but here the response is an oracle of judgment. This is not due to Yahweh ignoring the lament and pleas for help, but rather because the prophet's plea is in reality an appeal for God to display his justice and righteousness by sending judgment where it belongs.

5–6. The prophet and people together are called to look in amazement among the *nations*,[2] where an unprecedented event is about to take place by the hand of God. The subject *I* is

[1] See Johnson, 'Paralysis of the Torah', pp. 257–266.
[2] The LXX, and therefore Acts 13:41, reads 'Oh scoffers'; *cf.* Hab. 1:13; 2:5, where this proposed word occurs in the MT. The variation between the two Heb. words is slight, and there is no compelling reason to alter the text here. See 1:6, where the same word occurs as in the Heb. of this verse in the singular, building the literary development of the oracle which would be sacrificed if the text were emended.

supplied from verse 6 by the LXX and several English translations. The two initial verbs in the verse, *look* and *watch*, associate Yahweh's response directly with Habakkuk's lament, where the same two verbs are used (1:3). The surprising event is God's raising from among the surrounding peoples *that ruthless and impetuous people*, a nation known for its ferocity and impulsiveness (*cf.* Jdg. 18:25). This apparently refers to the swift rise to power of the 'Chaldeans' (AV, RSV, NEB, JB; *Babylonians*, NIV; see p. 44), who are described in the rest of this section.

Their widespread dispossession of peoples throughout 'the breadth of the earth' (RSV), *i.e.* the Fertile Crescent, was for the purpose of acquiring property *not their own*, a word play on two Hebrew homonyms (*i.e.* like-sounding words'), *lō'* and *lô*.

7. The effect of the Babylonians on those with whom they came into contact was terror and *dread* (AV, NIV), a word usually used to describe the awesome response to God himself by one who experienced his presence (*cf.* Ex. 34:10; Dt. 7:21; Zp. 2:11; Mal. 1:14). The Babylonians were arrogant, setting themselves up in God's place even as far as promulgating their own *law* and honouring themselves (*cf.* Gn. 49:3; Ho. 13:1; see v. 11b). Power and pride often go together.

8–9. The might of her *cavalry* is compared to the *leopard* and the 'night wolf' (AV, RSV; *cf.* Zp. 3:3)[1] in their fleetness[2] and ferocity. Their approaching gallop (JB, NIV)[3] *from afar* (see v. 6, *cf.* Is. 39:3) is compared to the swoop of an 'eagle' (RSV; *vulture*, NIV; *cf.* Jb. 9:26; Je. 4:13; La. 4:19) in its voracity and purposeful *violence*.

The middle clause of verse 9 is obscure, with the meaning of two of its three words debated. In the context of advancing armies it appears to speak of *hordes* (NIV; 'sea of faces', NEB; 'totality, all', Holladay[4]) whose 'faces' are set to *advance*. The last word has also been interpreted as the 'east wind' which comes from the hot desert regions and scorches the land (so the NIV, which thus uses two possible meanings for the same word; *cf.* JB). The dessicating wind motif has validity here

---

[1] An alteration of vocalization results in 'wolves of the plain/desert' (*cf.* Je. 5:6) or 'Arabia' (LXX).

[2] DSS reads 'voice', due to a simple scribal transposition of two letters.

[3] A rare Heb. word of uncertain meaning.

[4] W. L. Holladay, *A Concise Hebrew and Aramaic Lexicon of the Old Testament* (Wm. B. Eerdmans, 1971), p. 182.

because it is used elsewhere to symbolize devastation from the east (*cf.* Je. 18:17; Ho. 12:1; 13:15) and explicitly from Babylon (Ezk. 17:10). It is also appropriate to the simile which immediately follows and is picked up again in verse 11. The grammatical form is, however, difficult.

The voracious Babylonians *gather prisoners* as their prey in their military advances. So numerous are they that they are as uncountable as the *sand*. The simile would have added power, since it is most often used in a positive sense of blessing and of a mighty military power (*cf.* Gn. 32:12; 41:49; Is. 48:19 and Jos. 11:4; Jdg. 7:12; 1 Sa. 13:5). Here the metaphor is turned on its head; instead of its usual positive force, one finds it in the context of Judah's defeat. This is part of the surprising response to Habakkuk's prayer regarding violence (vv. 2–3) – more violence. It is an example of *lex talionis*, the punishment fitting the crime (*cf.* Gn. 9:6; Lv. 24:19–20; Ps. 7:16).

10–11. The relative power of the arrogant nation is shown by their ability to *scoff* at *kings* and 'princes' (JB); the *rulers* of other nations are objects of ridicule. Not only is the leadership of others contemptible, so also are their fortifications; their *fortified cities* are breached by laying *earthern ramps* against the walls (*cf.* 2 Sa. 20:15; Ezk. 4:2).[1] After a defeat by siege, the cavalry (vv. 8–9) are able to continue their progress, sweeping along *like the wind* (RSV, NEB, NIV, *BHS* mg.).[2]

The last clause is grammatically difficult, but it takes note of the already mentioned arrogant pride of the Babylonians (v. 7), in that they deify their *own strength*, thereby making themselves *guilty*,[3] a common fault among major powers who attribute their position on the world stage to their own doings (*cf.* Is. 47:8, 10; Zp. 2:15).

---

[1] See Y. Yadin, *The Art of Warfare in Biblical Lands* (McGraw–Hill, 1963) and the pictures in J. B. Pritchard (ed.), *The Ancient Near East*, 1 (Princeton University Press, 1958), illustration 101.

[2] In Hebrew the word is an accusative indicating manner, *cf.* G–K 118, r. The JB reads 'wind' as the subject, which is possible, being a symbol of Babylon's sweeping power (*cf.* v. 9), though 'wind' is generally, though not invariably, feminine in Hebrew, while the verb here is masculine.

[3] The recapitulation is lost with the DSS reading of 'he set up his altar to his god'.

IV. THE PROBLEM OF EXCESSIVE PUNISHMENT
(1:12–17)

Habakkuk takes up another lament psalm (see vv. 2–4) when he hears Yahweh's response. He starts with the character of God in his holiness and justice (vv. 12–13a) and then questions God's mode of punishment in the light of his character (vv. 13b–17). His confidence in God is shown not only in the psalm's first verse, but also in the verse which follows the psalm (2:1), in which he patiently awaits the response to his plea.

12. The section opens with a rhetorical question (see the Additional Note on rhetorical questions, p. 29) that expects an affirmative answer. Israelite faith held that Yahweh was *from everlasting* (*cf.* Dt. 33:27; Ps. 55:19). Not only God's eternity but also his active involvement in Israel's history is shown by the use of his covenant name Yahweh (*cf.* Ex. 6:2–8). This Great One is personalized and made close when he is called *my God* (*cf.* Pss. 3:7; 7:1), a real God of objective power rather than the subjective deification of their own strength 'worshipped' by the Babylonians (v. 11). This God is characterized as *my Holy One*. His holiness provides the very basis upon which one can come to him for help (see Ps. 22:3). Because of him and his character, the prophet, and Israel whom he represents, *will not die*,[1] lest the covenant be broken.

Yahweh is called *Rock* (*cf.* Dt. 32:18; Ps. 19:14), indicating his changeless stability. He 'established' (RSV) the Babylonian nation for a purpose, namely for *judgment* and 'chastisement' (RSV). The prophet thus claims that God's creative power raises up and uses even nations who do not recognize him as God. The first purpose is intentionally chosen to counter Habakkuk's lament in 1:4, which arose from the apparent lack of justice. In reality, justice and redemptive correction (*cf.* Jb. 5:17; Pr. 3:12) are established by God himself, no matter which instrument he chooses to bring them about.

13. The recital of God's attributes continues by detailing his purity, a complete separation from sin and evil. Israel's purification laws were to ritually cleanse themselves from

---

[1] Rabbinic tradition sees this verb as an example of scribal emendation, changing the unthinkable 'you shall die' (see *IDBS*, pp. 263–264). There is no manuscript evidence for the change, and arguments for it are not compelling.

defilement due to external contact with uncleanness (see Lv. 11 – 12; 15; Nu. 19), though cleanliness of the heart from sin is the ultimate goal (see Ps. 51:7; Ezk. 36:25; Heb. 1:3; 9:14). This is necessitated by God's complete abhorrence of evil, here specified metaphorically in reference to his *eyes*, which are unable to countenance *evil* and *wrong* (Ps. 5:4–5). The verbs (*look* and *tolerate*) and the second verbal object (*wrong*) used here are picked up from the first lament in verse 3. The prophet's faith in a holy God is challenged by the reality of Yahweh's choice of the Babylonians as an instrument of punishment. This causes Habakkuk to again ask '*why*' (*cf.* 1:3).

The actual content of his moral problem is detailed in verses 13b–17. In general, it is countenancing the *treacherous* (JB, NIV; 'wicked', NEB), who break relationships established with God or man. Here they parallel *the wicked* (see 1:4), who *swallow up* like voracious animals (*cf.* Ex. 7:12; Jon. 1:17) the nation of Judah, which, while sinning against God, is *more righteous* (*cf.* 1:4) than those who are the instruments of God's punishment upon them. 'The wicked' has changed its referent from the unfaithful of Israel to the Babylonians themselves (see pp. 45–46). What astonishes Habakkuk is that God is *silent* at this new, unjust turn of events (*cf.* Gn. 34:5; Est. 7:4; Ps. 50:21; Is. 42:14) – he ought, in the light of his character as understood by Habakkuk, to be doing something to right them.

14–15c. But not only does God allow evil to happen to the righteous (v. 13), he seems actively to make preparation for it, according to the imagery used here. God makes 'mankind' in its creational entirety, including Judah, to be *like fish* and 'crawling things' (RSV), prehuman creations of God (*cf.* Gn. 1:26, 28). They not only *have no ruler* from among themselves (*cf.* Pr. 6:7; 30:27), but are under the rule of others, namely man (*cf.* Gn. 9:2; Ps. 8:6–8).

The fish analogy is carried over to Babylon's treatment of Judah, violently 'dragging them out' (RSV; *cf.* Pr. 21:7) *with hooks* (*cf.* Jb. 41:1; Is. 19:8; Am. 4:2) and *net* (*cf.* Ec. 7:26; Ezk. 32:3; Mi. 7:2), and gathering (1:9) by 'seine' (RSV; *cf.* Ps. 141:10; Is. 19:8; 51:20), symbolic of judgment and conquest not only in the Old Testament but also in the ancient Near East, where one finds depictions of defeated captives taken into nets.[1] Wresting captives from their own environment, their native land, and exiling or transplanting them into a foreign region was a common practice among the Assyrians and the Babylonians (see 2 Ki. 17:5–6, 24; 24:12–16; 25:11–12, 18–21). This separation from one's homeland quenched the fires of rebellion which might still smoulder, since one would not be likely to fight for the liberation of a country not one's own.

15d–16. As a result of being able to exploit the Judaeans like fish, Babylon *rejoices* and *is glad*. Often, though not exclusively, the grounds for such a response are God and his actions (*cf.* 3:18; Ps. 9:14; 32:11). Here the Babylonian's pride (1:7, 11) leads him to rejoice in himself. As part of this rejoicing and self-arrogation, he deifies his *net* (v. 15) and *sacrifices* and *burns incense* to it. The particular forms of the two verbs found here are often used of false idolatrous worship (*e.g.* 1 Ki. 11:8; 12:32; Ps. 106:38; Ho. 11:2 – sacrifice; Jer. 44:23; Am. 4:5 – incense), though not always (*e.g.* 1 Ki. 8:5; 2 Chr. 30:22 – sacrifice; 1 Sam. 2:16 – incense). Each time the two verbs are used together, it is invariably involving pagan worship in almost a fixed formula of condemnation (*cf.* 2 Ki. 12:3; 14:4; 2 Ch. 28:4; Ho. 4:13; 11:2). Therefore, simply by his choice of words, Habakkuk is condemning the Babylonian practice. To these nets, rather than to Yahweh, were attributed Babylon's *luxury* (RSV, NIV, JB; lit. 'fatness, richness'; *cf.* Gn. 49:20, Is. 30:23) and 'rich food' (*cf.* RSV, NEB; also lit. 'fat'; Gn. 41:2; Jdg. 3:17; 'food' is resumed from 1:8).

17. The questioning of 1:13 is resumed[2] as to whether *he* (the Babylonian king or nation) will continue *emptying his net*[3] (see vv. 15–16) and still prosper from his oppression. What is continued is ambiguous. Grammatically it refers to the following verb, 'kill' (*cf.* AV, JB mg.), but a minor textual alteration, seeing an example of dittography or erroneous duplicating, results in the adverb referring to emptying nets (1QpHab, *BHS*, RSV, JB, NIV). The following mention of

---

[1] See Pritchard, *Ancient Near East*, 1, illustration 121 and O. Keel, *The Symbolism of the Biblical World* (Seabury, 1978), p. 90.

[2] 1QpHab reads this as a statement rather than a question, as do other versions, so either reading is textually possible, but the MT logically leads into 2:1, where a response is awaited.

[3] 1QpHab reads 'unsheathe his sword' (NEB), due to a very slight scribal misreading.

unmerciful, unsparing slaughter (AV, JB) is thus a summary of the literal treatment meted out by Babylon which was previously expressed in the fishing imagery.

V. AWAITING AN ANSWER (2:1)

In the light of his questions to God and his belief in God's faithfulness, Habakkuk, using military terminology, awaits God's response, 'what he might say'. He stands *watch* (*cf.* Is. 21:8; Ezk. 33:7), taking up his position in order to keep alert (*cf.* Ps. 5:3; Mi. 7:7) for God's response. This watchful vigilance is one of the roles of the prophet, who, like a sentry, is to guard against the departure of God's people or their leaders from the parameters of the covenant of God (*cf.* 2 Sa. 12; 1 Ki. 17 – 22; Am. 7:8–9). Habakkuk, however, looks in the other direction. He waits to see how God will act in the light of the stipulation found in the covenant, to which he also is a signatory, that sin necessitates punishment (Dt. 28:15–68). Not only does the prophet await God's answer, he waits to see how he himself will react, how he himself 'will answer' (RSV) in the dialogue with God. A proposed emendation, without textual support, and thus with little merit, reads this as seeking how God himself will answer (*cf. BHS*).

VI. YAHWEH'S SECOND RESPONSE (2:2–20)

In the light of Habakkuk's questions regarding the fitness of using a violent, pagan instrument to punish God's people, Yahweh tells of the pending destruction of Babylon. He does this through a vision (vv. 2–3) which includes five songs that taunt or deride the Chaldeans.

A. A vision (2:2–5)

i. Announcement (2:2–3). Yahweh answers Habakkuk, as he expected (v. 1) – not, however, for the benefit of the prophet alone, but also for the information of others. Habakkuk is told to *write down* the 'vision' (RSV; *revelation*, NIV) clearly so that it might be preserved and transmitted, since its message will not take immediate effect (*cf.* Is. 30:8). It would happen in its *appointed time* (AV, NEB, NIV), one chosen by God, and not before. God's purpose is unfolding sequentially and in order in the course of historical events. History is not cyclical, a constant recurrence of events in futile repetition, but rather it is linear. It is moving towards the goal of the Day of the Lord and the establishment of God's kingdom. Specific historical events or appointed moments such as this are especially significant in the progression towards this final objective. Though this message of God might not reach fruition immediately, Habakkuk is certain that it will take effect at the time of God's own choosing.

The message is to be written on *tablets*, the usual medium of Babylonian writing, though not unknown in Israel (*cf.* Ex. 24:12; Dt. 4:13; 1 Ki. 8:9). The choice of medium is apparently due to its durability, necessitated by the possible delay in fulfilment. It is written 'in order that the one who reads it may run', but the interpretation of this is uncertain. It could involve passers-by, who will be able to read the message as they go by and then pass the message on informally to those they meet, or it could mean *a herald*, whose specific function will be to spread the message throughout the land (so NEB, NIV). In the context of harsh Babylonian oppression and the resultant despondency of God's people, this must be an invigorating message of hope which revives the downcast to *run*, as God's power and presence does in another passage concerning comfort in face of the Babylonian might (see Is. 40:31).

The content of the message is not explicitly stated, but it must contain hope for those who read it. Various suggestions have been proposed as to its content,[1] but none are certain. Perhaps the entire prophecy now found in Habakkuk is in view, a message of hope for God's people arising from his very nature.[2]

The prophet is to restrain his impatience (*cf.* 1:2) and *wait* for God to act in his own way and time, as one can wait for judgment (*cf.* Zp. 3:8) or blessing (*cf.* Ps. 33:20; Is. 64:4). Even if delayed, the 'fulfilment' (JB; *end*, NIV) of God's word is sure (*cf.* 2 Pet. 3:3–9).

ii. Life and death (2:4–5). The triumph of faithfulness is

---

[1] See Johnson, 'Paralysis of the Torah', p. 259.
[2] See 1:1, where the same Heb. root is used to describe the book.

contrasted with the arrogant restlessness and lack of fulfilment of those who do not rely on God. The centrality of faith is picked up in the New Testament (*cf.* Rom. 1:17; Gal. 3:11; Heb. 10:38), and became the goad which prompted Luther to re-examine his own theology (see p. 48), with momentous consequences for the Reformation. It also provided the answer for the moral problem posed in 1:13.

4. A contrast is made between the *righteous* (see 1:4, 13) and the unnamed one whose 'soul' (AV, JB; *desires*, NIV) is *not upright*, having deviated from the moral norm (*cf.* Dt. 12:8; Ps. 32:11; Is. 26:7). From the context, the latter is the Babylonian oppressors of Judah who have become *puffed up* (RSV mg., NIV) and arrogant[1] (*cf.* 1:7, 10–11). This Babylonian self-righteousness, seeking their own ends, not only leads to pride and the sinful acts of the next verses, it can also lead to death (*cf.* Pr. 14:12; 16:25). This death is their implied though unstated end, in contrast to the life which awaits the righteous. This desired preservation of life will come to Judah if they show *faith*, waiting in patient assurance that Yahweh will act as he promised in verse 3. While the odds might be strongly against them in the face of the seemingly all-powerful Babylon, God will vindicate his people by giving them life, both temporally (in contrast to the Babylonians who would soon disappear from the world stage, see p. 45), and eschatologically. In this context, therefore, the life promised is political and national, in contrast to the imminent national demise of the oppressor.

The Hebrew leaves some ambiguity as to whose faith or faithfulness is meant. The most straightforward reading is that adopted above, where the righteous are the subject, they show faith. Another interpretation has the faithfulness on God's part, life coming because of God's covenant promises to preserve his people. This reading could be what led the LXX to change the pronoun to 'my faith[fulness]' in this context of God addressing the prophet. Another LXX reading refers this pronoun to 'my righteous one' who will live due to faithfulness. Apparently this is so understood by the writer to the Hebrews, who encourages those dismayed by Christ's delayed return to persevere (Heb. 10:38), trusting God that the 'Coming One'

---

[1] See Nu. 14:44, where a verb of the same root indicates arrogant presumption. The feminine form of the Heb. word here could agree with 'soul', making the proposed emendation of *BHS* unnecessary.

(Heb. 10:37, a revocalization of Hab. 2:3[1]) will ultimately arrive. The idea of an impending arrival is shared by Habakkuk and Hebrews, but the more general message of the former is personalized as the Messiah in the latter.

There are two citations of this passage in Paul's epistles. In Romans 1:17 Paul discusses righteousness that is imputed or given by God (see NIV) only on the basis of faith. This is the gospel, the good news which is open to all (Rom. 1:16), that because one believes God, persuaded that his covenant promises are reliable (see Hab. 2:4), one is considered righteous (see Rom. 3:22; 4:11, 13; 5:1 and elsewhere) and is granted life. The ambiguity of the referent of the righteousness remains in the grammatical construction in Romans, but the context makes clear that it is here a gift of God rather than an attribute of God; it does not characterize him here, but is rather bestowed by him.

The ambiguity is even more clearly resolved in Galatians 3:11, because there Paul contrasts different possible sources of righteousness. Rather than self-righteousness, attempted through pious acts, namely 'the law' which justifies no-one (*i.e.* none are made righteous before God through observing it), the true source is faith, wholehearted commitment to the faithfulness of God. The referent is so clear that Paul does not even use a pronoun – it is simply faith, that of God's child in him, that is efficacious.

While potentially ambiguous in Habakkuk, the concept of the necessity of faith, a heart attitude rather than outward actions, is not foreign to the Old Testament (*cf.* Gn. 15:6; Am. 5:21–24). Therefore the gospel so diligently preached by Paul is as much a part of the old covenant as it is of the new. The false dichotomy of 'Old Testament = Law; New Testament = Grace' is seen in reality to be illusory.

5. After the interlude of living hope for the faithful (v. 4), Habakkuk looks again ('moreover', RSV) at their opponent, the *arrogant* (RSV, NIV; *cf.* Pr. 21:24), proud nation who revels in her own powers (*cf.* 1:7, 10–11, 16; 2:4). Babylon is drunk on *wine*, part of the spoils of war (*cf.* 1 Sa. 30:16; 1 Ki. 20:12,

---

[1] Instead of the MT's *bō' yābō'*, 'it will surely come', in 2:3b, Hebrews personalizes the form, revocalizing the infinitive as a participle (*bā' yābō'*, 'a coming one will come').

16; Is. 5:11–12, 22).[1] Her intoxication (both literal and figurative), with victory going to her head, while emboldening her 'heroes', actually enervates them and proves a 'traitor' (NEB; *cf.* Pr. 20:1; 23:21, 29–35; Is. 28:7). Babylon is associated with wine and drunkenness in other places (*cf.* Je. 51:7; Dn. 5:1–30). An aim of conquest is to find room to expand and settle one's flocks and herds so they can multiply. Babylon, however, will not be able to settle and 'find pasturage' (be *at rest*, NIV; 'abide', RSV),[2] so her goals will be foiled by God.

Next, in a series of four clauses, the first of which is a relative clause starting with 'who' (JB), the arrogant one is further described. He is voracious and 'insatiable' (NEB, JB; *never satisfied*, NIV; *cf.* Pr. 30:15–16; Is. 9:20; Ezk. 16:28–29), devouring his opponents like 'Sheol' (NEB, JB; *the grave*, NIV), the place of the dead (*cf.* Nu. 16:30; Ps. 49:14; Is. 5:14), and *like death* itself (*cf.* Pr. 27:20; Ezk. 31:14). This insatiability is identified as their conquest of *nations* and *peoples*, all of which are gathered like so much grain in the harvest (*cf.* Ex. 23:10; Dt. 11:14; Ru. 2:7). This desire for expansion and conquest, picked up from 1:15–17, is further elaborated, and condemned, in 2:6–17. This verse therefore serves as a transition to the next part of God's message to Habakkuk.

B. Taunting woes (2:6–20)

In a series of five separate oracles of woe, Babylon is mocked. Judah is not mourning the impending fall of her overlord, but uses the literary form of a dirge to ridicule her. Even though she looked invincible when Habakkuk was speaking, God's power would bring her low by 539 BC (see p. 45). Each oracle details the crimes perpetrated and the different responses to them.

i. The pillager (2:6–8). 6. As an introduction to the following oracles, the first line sets their tone as 'taunts' (see

---

[1] DSS reads 'wealth' which betrays (*cf.* JB), which fits the context of greed in this verse, but since 'wine' also makes good sense, there is no compelling reason to alter the text. Even less evidence exists for altering the text to 'woe' (*BHS*), a similar Heb. form used five times in the chapter (vv. 6, 9, 12, 15, 19).

[2] The verb is unique in the Bible, but nouns of the same root denote pasturage and places of residence (*cf.* 2 Sa. 7:8; Ps. 23:2; Is. 32:18; Je. 10:25; Am. 1:2). These will be denied to Babylon.

RSV, NIV). The three words used here as *taunt, ridicule* and *scorn* are more often used in wisdom literature and teaching. Therefore Babylonia serves here as a proverbial kind of object lesson of those who overstep God's bounds.

The first oracle proper starts in verse 6b with a characteristic *woe* which is found in each of the other four (vv. 9, 12, 15, 19). This is often used in funeral dirges (*cf.* 1 Ki. 13:30; Je. 22:18; 34:5; 48:1), of which these are parodies (see also Is. 14 which, while not including 'woe', is called a taunt, v. 4).[1]

The first woe is directed towards those who acquire goods dishonestly. Both means of acquisition involve word plays in the Hebrew, being one of the characteristics of Hebrew wisdom sayings (see v. 6a). The first involves one 'amassing' (JB) goods which are not his, either through robbery or fraud. The word play involves homonymy (see 1:6).[2] The second means is *extortion* through accumulation of 'pledges' (RSV; NEB; JB; *cf.* Dt. 24:10–13). These are items used as security in case of default on a loan. They too often were confiscated prematurely or without thought for the needs of the borrower. This practice at times led to enslavement of the poor who needed to borrow money (*cf.* Ne. 5:1–5), since the last pledge or surety which could be offered and forfeited would be oneself. 'Pledge' can be read as a combination of two Hebrew words signifying a 'cloud of dust' (see 'thick clay', AV; DSS), a word play on the impurity of sin and the clinging mire that forced indebtedness leads to, a state from which one is not easily extricated. The heinousness of the extortion is indicated by the shocked cry *how long*, when will it cease?

7. The punishment fits the crime and the *victim* (NEB, JB, NIV) will become victor. The extortion will become so great that they will finally and *suddenly* shake off their apathetic lethargy and themselves 'shake' (NEB) the oppressor. The victims are defined as *debtors*, referring to the exploited poor in verse 6b who have been charged exorbitant interest (*cf.* Dt. 23:19–20). A literal reading of the concept of interest here is 'putting the bite on' someone, a concept and idiom unfortunately all too familiar today.

8. The tit-for-tat relationship between crime and punish-

---

[1] For a more detailed comparison of these two passages, see D. E. Gowan, *The Triumph of Faith in Habakkuk* (John Knox Press, 1976), pp. 61–62.

[2] A play on the similar sound of different words, here *lō' lô*.

ment is explicitly noted by the plundering of the plunderers. All who have been hurt and have survived, even if only as a 'remnant' (AV, RSV), including the debtors of verse 7, will arise against the destroyers of lands and peoples. This could involve literal violence and bloodshed, or the practice of usury could be metaphorically compared to drawing blood, as it is in contemporary usage.

ii. The plotter (2:9–11). The second oracle condemns not only exploitation for personal gain, but also for national or dynastic aggrandizement.

9. This *woe* (see v. 6) is directed towards those who seek *gain*, not because this is wrong in itself, since the concept is morally neutral (*cf.* Jb. 22:3; Ps. 30:9 [Heb. v.10]; Mi. 4:13b; Mal. 3:14), but because it is often done in a way which is *unjust* (NEB, NIV; 'evil', AV, RSV; *cf.* 1 Sa. 8:3; Pr. 1:19; Je. 6:13). A word play is based on the repetition of the same Hebrew root,[1] which can literally be translated by the contemporary colloquialism of 'taking one's cut'. The national guilt for this sin is shown by its beneficiary being one's 'house' (AV, RSV, JB) or 'dynasty'. There is a word play on this meaning of royal succession and on the other common use as a physical dwelling (*cf.* 2 Sa. 7:5, 11, 16 and the current English usage of 'house'). Their dwelling-place will be rendered invulnerable, like a high *nest* (*cf.* Nu. 24:21; Jb. 39:27–28; Ob. 4), in order that they might 'be safe' from every kind of 'evil' (AV; *ruin*, NIV) which they sought to inflict.

10–11. Rather than achieving its arrogantly intended invulnerability (v. 9), the plot, which sought to 'annihilate' other peoples, cutting off (*cf.* RSV) their very life and existence in order to exploit their lands and holdings, will bring shame to the very 'dynasty' (*house, cf.* v. 9) for which the injustices were committed.

Seeking to harm others puts their own *life* in jeopardy. The verb *ḥāṭā* used here (translated *forfeiting* in NIV) conveys the idea of being at fault due to some lack (*cf.* Pr. 8:36) and its resultant guilt (*cf.* Gn. 43:9; 1 Ki. 8:46). Even inanimate creation, the very building material of the intended 'house' (see vv. 9–10), will cry out in protest at the injustice perpetrated for its benefit (*cf.* Je. 22:13–17).

[1] *bōṣēaʿ beṣaʿ.*

iii. The promoter of violence (2:12–14). 12. The very foundations of the centres of society are founded on *bloodshed* (NEB, NIV, *cf.* v. 8; Na. 3:1, specifically referring to Nineveh; Mi. 3:10, to Jerusalem) and 'wickedness' (*cf.* Is. 59:3; Mi. 3:10). The forms used here are verbal adjectives, showing that the actions are not unique but characterize those who perform them.

13. The punishment description here is either borrowed from, or echoed in, the contemporary prophecy of Jeremiah (Je. 51:58), where it also refers to the impending destruction of Babylon. All of the effort of building and self-aggrandizement will be of no lasting value and will literally go up in smoke. These judgments are sure, arising as they do from 'Yahweh of hosts', God the warrior, who fights on behalf of his people (3:8–15; *cf.* 1 Sa. 17:45; 2 Ch. 20:15–17; Is. 47:4).

14. The gloom of the preceding and following woes is broken by a ray of light shining in the midst of the darkness of self-seeking. Not only will Judah's oppressor, the avaricious Babylon, be judged, but the *knowledge*, understanding and acknowledgment of Yahweh and of his presence will fill *the earth* (*cf.* Nu. 14:21; Is. 6:3), permeating every place like *water*. Theoretical knowledge is not sufficient, but rather an intimate encounter with the covenant God resulting in ethical living (*cf.* Pss. 36:10; 91:14; Pr. 3:5–6; contrast Is. 1:3–4; Ho. 4: 1–2, 16). This verse, a modified quotation from the description of the peaceful Messianic kingdom of Isaiah (Is. 11:9), raises the oracle from a single reference to Babylon's defeat and places it on the level of eschatology. In the last days God will move powerfully, bringing his kingdom to all creation. The violence of Babylon will ultimately be replaced by God's tranquillity, which will be universally enjoyed. The specific aspect of Yahweh which is highlighted, though not mentioned in the Isaianic original, is his *glory*, the outward aspect of God's being, his royal majesty and awesome power (*cf.* Ex. 40:34; Ps. 63:2) – the unlimited God in contrast to limited, grasping humanity. The ultimate triumph of this powerful God over wicked man starting here is detailed further in chapter 3.

iv. The debaucher (2:15–17). 15. Babylon is now condemned for leading others, her *neighbours*, into debauchery by causing them to drink intoxicants. The second Hebrew clause is textually difficult, seeming to mix an address to

Babylon with one to Yahweh, since it reads 'he who pours out your wrath', a form always associated with God's anger in judgment (*cf.* Ps. 79:6; Je. 10:25), which does not fit the context here. The text from Qumran reads 'his wrath', referring to the Babylonians, the subject of the immediate context. Some have interpreted the clause as erroneously duplicating one letter, a simple scribal error, which, when deleted, results in causing to drink '[from] the cup' (RSV; *wineskin*, NIV), a word associated elsewhere with intoxication (*cf.* Zc. 12:2). While not having textual support, it fits the context well.

The purpose of leading others into drunkenness is pruriently to catch sight of 'their nakedness' (AV, JB). Exhibiting someone in this state was a form of punishment (*cf.* the commentary on Na. 3:5, p. 37, and the references there). Inadvertent observation of nakedness and the lack of a respectful response to it were strongly dealt with in the case of Noah and his son Ham (Gn. 9:22–27), where inebriation also played a part (Gn. 9:21). The Babylonians' condemnation is greater since their action was deliberate rather than inadvertent.

16. As a fitting penalty for seeking to degrade her neighbours, Babylon will *be filled with shame* (*cf.* RSV). She was seeking to glorify herself by demeaning others, but this will not happen, since the nation will *drink* (see v. 15) and, in intoxication, reveal its own nakedness (so AV, JB, NIV). An inversion of two Hebrew letters results rather in Babylonia staggering (RSV, NEB, NIV mg.),[1] which makes logical sense and also has some manuscript support (Qumran, LXX, Syr., Vulg.; *cf.* Zc. 12:2). The latter interpretation gains support by the juxtaposition of forms of the Hebrew word with a *cup* of Yahweh (Is. 51:17, 22; *cf.* Zc. 12:2). While Babylon used a literal cup of intoxicant, Yahweh uses a figurative cup, extended by his own *right hand*. This contains God's wrath and judgment (*cf.* Ps. 75:8; La. 4:21; Ezk. 23:33; Lk. 22:42). The verse concludes by rewording its opening clause with a word play on Babylon's 'shame' (RSV, NEB).[2] An alternative reading of this last word allows a possible interpretation associated with 'vomit' (see AV),[3] a natural result of overdrinking (*cf.* Je. 25:27).

17. Babylon perpetrated *violence* (see 1:9) not only upon

---

[1] *vᵉhēʿārēl* (MT) to be read *vᵉhērāʾēl*.
[2] *qālôn* at the start of the verse and *qîqālôn* here.
[3] Reading *qîʾ qālôn*, 'vomiting of shame'.

Judah but also upon other conquered nations, including *Lebanon*, which historically would have felt her cruel heel after the battle of Carchemish in 605 BC (see p. 44). Lebanon, famed for her lush vegetation and mighty forests (*cf.* Ps. 72:16; Ho. 14:5–7), could well be used here metaphorically, saying that the Babylonians even went as far as denuding lands of their tree covering. This metaphorical understanding is supported by the context, since Babylon is also said to extend her savagery beyond shedding *man's blood* to the destruction of *animals* and even of the earth itself. Not only interhuman atrocities but also ecological excesses receive condemnation.

v. The pagan idolator (2:18–20). Babylon seeks her own well-being not only through violence and plunder, but also through resorting to impotent idols. The form of the oracle diverges slightly from the previous four in that the specific 'woe' clause comes in the middle (v. 19) rather than at the beginning (vv. 6, 9, 12, 15). There is no manuscript support for reversing the order of verses 18 and 19, as suggested by the JB. Here the futility of resorting to idols is judicially demonstrated in their inability to help.

18–19. The Babylonians, in order to seek revelation and guidance from the divine, devised *idols*. Three separate words are used for the false, man-made gods, although by this time original differences in nuance might have blurred. The first two concern their manner of construction, those *carved* (AV, NIV) from wood or stone (2 Ki. 21:7; Is. 45:20) and those cast from metal (Ex. 32:4, 8; Lv. 19:4; *cf.* Is. 40:19). The third word is a play on the ordinary word for Israel's God (*'elōhîm*), in which they are called *'elîlîm*, literally 'worthless things' (Je. 14:14; *cf.* Jb. 13:4; Zc. 11:17). These objects, expected to provide oracular guidance, are in reality 'dumb' (RSV). One who *trusts* in them, calling on them for a response, will be disappointed, since they are without life or breath (*cf.* Ps. 135:15–17). Instead of finding a source for truth, one who approaches idols finds a 'teacher' of *lies* (*cf.* Is. 9:15), something that not only does not perform its intended function, but in fact leads its worshippers into error by leading them away from the true and self-revealing God (*cf.* 1 Cor. 12:2).

20. The true source of revelation, by contrast, is present where he has always been, *in his holy temple* (*cf.* Ps. 11:4; Mi. 1:2). Yahweh is approached in silence, a fitting response to his holiness and majesty, and a token of one's respect for his being – dependency upon his grace and submission to his will (*cf.* Ps. 46:10; Is. 41:1). This silence is requested not only of Judah but of *all the earth*, who will ultimately acknowledge God as the true giver of knowledge (*cf.* Ps. 22:27; Is. 2:2–3). This contrasts with the frenetic activity of man to create 'speaking' gods, and the tumultuous cries of worshippers to make dumb idols respond. Lifeless idols approached in clamour are silent, while the living God, approached in silence and reverence, speaks.

The verse provides a bridge to the next major section of the prophecy in that it turns to the positive, looking at God, after the negative, attention to Babylon's sin.

VII. HABAKKUK'S PSALM (3:1–19)

In the canonical form of the book, Habakkuk reacts to God's responses to his questions by offering a prayer. He glorifies God for his person (vv. 2, 3b, 4) and his actions in creation (vv. 3a, 5–15). In response to his experience of the presence of Yahweh, Habakkuk provides one of the most moving statements of faith and trust found in Scripture (vv. 16–19).

A. Musical notes (3:1, 19b)

The chapter is opened and closed by technical comments that find their close parallels in the collection of liturgical literature found in the Psalms and which indicate that at some point it might have circulated separately from the remainder of the book (see p. 46). It is called a *prayer*, a word which heads lament or petition psalms (Pss. 17:1; 86:1; 90:1; 102:1; 142:1; *cf.* Ps. 72:20). Habakkuk is credited as being the author, or at least as having some association with the psalm's preservation (see 1:1). The psalm is also said to be *on shigionoth* ('dirge', JB), a rare term (Ps. 7:1) used only in cases of complete reliance on God's faithfulness. It is played on *stringed instruments* (Pss. 4:1; 6:1; 54:1; 55:1; 67:1; 76:1), possibly a harp (*cf.* 1 Sa. 16:16–23), and is under the leadership of a musical professional, a person figuring in fifty-five other psalm headings.

Another notation (*selāh*), unique to psalmic literature, is found three times in the chapter (vv. 3, 9, 13). It is probably a musical or liturgical instruction, but its meaning is not known.

B. Petition (3:2)

Based on the 'report' (RSV) of what Yahweh has done in the past, the psalmist responds in two ways. *I stand in awe* ('fear', RSV) shows his personal reaction to the power and sovereignty of the creating and sustaining God (*cf.* Gn. 22:12; Ps. 15:4; Pr. 1:7; Is. 50:10), whom he can but trust and obey. Some reverse the order of two Hebrew letters, resulting in the psalmist 'seeing' God's work (*cf.* NEB, *BHS*), but manuscript support for the change is slight. In addition to awe, the writer hopes that the One who acted mightily in the past (*cf.* 1:12) will do so in the present, now, 'in the midst of the years' (RSV), by fulfilling the promises of chapters 1 – 2. The past acts are to be 'revived' (*renewed*, RSV, NIV) so that God and his works might again be made *known* (*cf.* 2:14).[1] This 'work' (RSV) of Yahweh in history is described in verses 3–15 in terms of power and judgment.

Thundering *wrath* and judgment are not the total essence of God, even though they comprise part of the revelation of his being and reflect his attitude towards those who break his covenant, and so are inevitable in the prophet's current context of a wicked nation (see 1:2–4). He is also a God showing *mercy* towards those who obey his laws (*cf.* Ex. 34:6; Dt. 4:31; 30:3). In the midst of the punishment heaped on the opponents of God and his law, whether his own people (*cf.* 1:2–4) or their enemies (*cf.* 2:2–20), Habakkuk calls on God to *remember* and exhibit the merciful side of his character as well. This term is used elsewhere of God's covenant grace to people who acknowledge him (*cf.* Gn. 8:1; 9:15; Ne. 1:8; Jb. 14:13; Lk. 1:54, 72). The love of God is so strong that even when he is flagrantly ignored, deserted or rejected, he is drawn, as a husband to his wife, or a mother to her child, to

---

[1] The LXX gives rise to the tradition of the animals surrounding the manger at Bethlehem when it apparently reads 'in the middle of two living creatures (*sh*e*nayim ḥayyîm*) you will be known' instead of 'in the midst of years it will be revived (*shānîm ḥayyêhû*), in the midst of years you will make known'. This results from alternative interpretations of vocalization and the elision of two repeated words, but the Heb. is perfectly acceptable and does not require emendation.

love in spite of the actions of the other (*cf.* Is. 1:2, 18–20; Ho. 11:8–11). The wrongs are real, but so too are the compassion and the desire to forgive, if the 'condition' for restoration – a renewed desire to acknowledge God – is present to allow the floods of his mercy to be unleashed. This mercy is described in the last part of the psalm (vv. 16–19). So verse 2 thus serves as an encapsulation of the message of the book, and as a prayer all today need to make to the ever-just but ever-compassionate God.

C. God's powerful presence in history (3:3–15)

God's power is expressed in this psalm in terms of two different manifestations of his character. His coming is described in the language of theophany, in which the approach and arrival of deity is pictured in terms of extraordinary natural phenomena (vv. 3–7; *cf.* Ex. 3:1–5; 19:16–19; 24:15–17; 1 Ki. 19:11–12). He is also described as the Divine Warrior who battles both against the elements and against the enemies of his people for the sake of his name and of his kingdom (vv. 8–15; *cf.* Ex. 15:1–18; Pss. 24:7–10; 68; Is. 34:1–15; 51:9–10). The two motifs are blended in the psalm through the vocabulary and the historical allusions used.

i. God's coming (3:3–7). From his position in the middle of Israelite history (see v. 2), the psalmist looks back to God's mighty actions at the Exodus and ponders the future.

3–4. God's coming is first expressed in terms reminiscent of the theophany at Mt Sinai. *God*, using the old poetic form *'elôah* (*cf.* Dt. 32:15,17, and esp. Job, where it occurs over forty times), is described as the *Holy One* (*cf.* 1:12), a form associated elsewhere with God's power in the Exodus (*cf.* Lv. 11:44–45). He is 'coming' (jb; *cf.* neb) from *Teman*, a site in Edom or Seir (*cf.* Je. 49:7, 20; Ob. 9) and from *Mount Paran*, also in Edomite territory (*cf.* Gn. 21:21; Nu. 10:12; 12:16). This area of Edom/Seir, and specifically Paran, has strong associations with Yahweh's advance to help Israel in Exodus and conquest (*cf.* Dt. 33:2; Jdg. 5:4–5).

The outward manifestations of God's being are detailed as they would have been perceived by those who saw his advance. The light of his glory is described as 'radiance' (neb; *glory*, av, rsv, niv; *cf.* Jb. 37:22; 40:10; Ps. 104:1–2), 'shining' (*cf.* Pr. 4:18; Is. 60:3) in twin *rays*[1] (*cf.* Ex. 34:29–30, 35). The latter word is also used of 'horns' (AV; *cf.* 1 Sa. 16:13; 1 Ki. 22:11), which are themselves a symbol of strength and *power* (*cf.* 1 Sa. 2:10; La. 2:3,17), which is also found in these verses. This could be a deliberate play on these two meanings, tying in the brilliance of God's coming with his mighty power which is yet to be detailed. This splendour, and the *praise* to which it gives rise, fills all of creation (*the heavens* and *the earth*; *cf.* Gn. 1:1; Ps. 104:2–5).

5. God is accompanied in his advance by *plague* and *pestilence*. These were associated with the Exodus (*cf.* Ex. 9:3,15; Ps. 78:48,50) and God's meeting with Israel at Mt Sinai (*cf.* Ex. 5:3; Nu. 14:12). In the ancient Near East, important people were accustomed to being accompanied by attendants (*cf.* 1 Sa. 17:7; 2 Sa. 15:1). So here Yahweh has his two personified attendants who are subject to his control (*cf.* Ps. 91:6), exemplifying his power. Both are also Canaanite deities, leading here to a hidden polemic against pagan worship, since these are not self-existent divine beings, but rather physical manifestations acting under Yahweh's orders (*cf.* this same sort of 'demythologizing' of luminary deities in Gn. 1:16).

6. As nature was convulsed at Sinai when Yahweh met with his people (Ex. 19:16–19), so his approach now will lead to earthquake[2] and fearful trembling (*cf.* Jb. 37:1) among the *nations*. This widens far beyond the specific events of the Exodus and wilderness wanderings, since the affected *hills* and *mountains* are *eternal* and everlasting (*cf.* Gn. 49:26; Dt. 33:15). They symbolize age-old permanence which will be disturbed by the God who is truly permanent and 'everlasting' (RSV, NEB, JB; *cf.* Ps. 90:2) in all of his *ways*. This verse moves into the cosmic and eschatological aspects of Yahweh's coming (*cf.* Ps. 97:4–5; Is. 29:6; Joel 3:16; Na. 1:5; Zc. 14:4; Rev. 16:18). It moves from a unique experience of God when he brought his people out of Egypt to a declaration about God's character, the way he is for all time, and so will be again.

7. The theophany in this section closes as it began, looking to the south (see v. 3), to two peoples who would have been the first to perceive God's coming from that direction. These bedouin nomads, characterized by *tents*, are *Cushan* and *Midian*.

---

[1] The Heb. grammatical form indicating duality.

[2] The word 'collapsed' is unique, while 'crumbled' is used in other forms of 'shattering' (Jb. 16:12; Je. 23:29).

The former is unknown outside this passage, but could be an alternative name or could indicate a subgroup of the Midianites, nomads of the Sinai and Negev regions (*cf.* Gn. 37:28, 36; Ex. 2:15; 3:1; Nu. 22:4, 7). The reason for the emotional *anguish* of these people is injustice, if the first words of the verse are understood as meaning 'because of (*cf.* 2 Sa. 19:22) injustice', *i.e.* the wrongdoing of the people which the prophet observes. This interpretation, which takes *'āven* to mean 'injustice' and not *distress* (NIV; see 1:3 where it is used in this sense) is valid, but does not appear to fit the context and is therefore not reflected in the English versions. Since sin is not mentioned in the theophany, and these peoples do not appear, much less receive condemnation, anywhere else in the book, many scholars revocalize the first two Hebrew words to express terror (*cf. BHS*, RSV, JB, NIV).[1] This accords well with the context, and is certainly a cause of anguish.

ii. God's combat (3:8–15). This is a new section, since Yahweh is addressed directly in the second person 'you' rather than simply being the subject of the discussion. The imagery also changes, for God is here presented as the Divine Warrior. He is one whose actions lead to fear, as did his very being in the previous verses (vv. 3–7). This and the preceding passage are united by common references to events of the period of the Exodus, Sinai and the Conquest.

8. Yahweh, the addressee, first confronts *sea* and *rivers* in *wrath* and anger. In Canaanite mythology, Baal had confronted the personified god Yam (sea), alternatively called Judge River.[2] Israel borrowed this motif but dropped any idea that natural phenomena are personified deities. Yahweh is presented as having engaged in combat with the sea at creation or at other unspecified periods (*cf.* Jb. 26:12–13; Pss. 29; 89:9–10). The same motif is also picked up and used in the context of God's mighty acts of salvation in the Exodus and Conquest, when the Red Sea and Jordan were parted through God's power (*cf.* Ex. 13:17–14:31; Jos. 3:13–17; 4:21–24; Is. 10:26; 43:16; 50:2). *Horses* and *chariots* are associ-

---

[1] *tahat 'āven* ('because of injustice') to *tēḥāte'nâ* or *tᵉḥitteynâ* ('in terror'); *cf.* Akkadian *ḫa'attu*, 'panic, terror' (Oppenheim, *Assyrian Dictionary*, 6, p. 1) and *ḫattu*, 'panic, fear' (*ibid.*, p. 150).

[2] See M. D. Coogan, *Stories from Ancient Canaan* (Westminster Press, 1978), pp. 75–115.

ated with the Red Sea event (*cf.* Ex. 14:5–28; Dt. 11:4; Jos. 24:6), only here in Habakkuk they are part of God's own army (*cf.* 2 Ki. 2:11–12; Je. 4:13; Zc. 6:1–7; Rev. 9:7–9; 19:11–21) rather than that of his enemies. They bring salvation for God's people rather than slaughter (see vv. 13, 18).

God's control over bodies of water is also an eschatological motif, showing his continued power over his creation (*cf.* Is. 11:15; Na. 1:4; Mt. 14:22–33; Rev. 21:1).

9a. More of God's arsenal joins the chariotry of verse 8. He readies his *bow* (a possible allusion to the flood, Gn. 9:13–16) and *arrows* (lit. 'staffs', see v. 14), taking them out of their 'sheath' (RSV). The adjective describing the arrows is ambiguous. The same root in Hebrew connotes 'swearing' (*cf.* AV) and the number 'seven', and both readings have some support. Sevenfold volleys were known in Israel's warfare,[1] although no evidence is found for the period under discussion. In Baal mythology, the deity's arrows are lightning (seven in number in one text[2]), so we could have here another echo from Canaanite poetry. Arrows used by Yahweh in punishment and judgment are common in poetry (*cf.* v. 11; Dt. 32:23; Pss. 7:13; 18:14). The concept of 'dedicating' the weapons, using the alternative meaning of the word 'seven', is also known in Israel (cf. Dt. 32:40–42) and appears to fit the context better. Here the dedication is done orally, by a 'word' (AV).

9b–11. The profound effect of the presence of the Divine Warrior on nature is graphically detailed. The *earth*'s surface is changed. It is *split* as at creation (*cf.* Ps. 74:15) and the time of the flood (Gn. 7:11) by *rivers*, as the waters themselves were split by God at the Red Sea (Ex. 14:16, 21; Ne. 9:11; Ps. 78:13; Is. 63:12). *Mountains . . . writhed* (RSV, NIV) like someone in terror or pain (*cf.* Dt. 2:25; Is. 26:18). This picture is also associated with the Red Sea crossing, where the *water* and the *deep* moved violently (Ps. 77:16), in *torrents* (NEB, NIV; *cf.* Ps. 77:17), as it does here with crashing noise and rising *waves* (Heb., 'hands', *cf.* AV).

---

[1] See G. Vermes, *The Dead Sea Scrolls in English* (Penguin Books, ²1975), pp. 131, 134.

[2] See J. Day, 'Echoes of Baal's Seven Thunders and Lightnings in Psalm XXIX and Habakkuk III 9 and the Identity of the Seraphim in Isaiah VI', *VT* 19 (1979), pp. 143–151, where he sees the seven lightnings here paralleling the seven thunders of God's voice in Ps. 29:3, 4a, 4b, 5, 7, 8, 9.

Celestial bodies are also affected by God's might. Instead of continuing their perpetual orbit, *sun* and *moon* stand, as they had done under God's command at one point during the conquest under Joshua (Jos. 10:12–14; *cf.* 2 Ki. 20:9–11; Is. 38:8). In this case, they remain in their 'habitation' (AV, RSV), a term usually used of God's dwelling-place, the Temple (1 Ki. 8:13; Is. 63:15). This is the opposite of the events of Joshua, where sunshine was prolonged (*cf.* the NEB and NIV, which interpret this as continued light). Darkness, rather than light, is a sign of God's powerful presence (Dt. 4:11; 2 Sa. 22:12) and of judgment (Joel 2:31; *cf.* Ex. 10:21–22; Ezk. 32:8). In the presence of the mighty Warrior, the only sources 'for light' are God's *arrows* and *spear*, the *lightning* (*cf.* Pss. 18:14–15; 77:17–18; 144:6; Zc. 9:14) which flashes in theophanies (*cf.* Ex. 19:16) and also in judgment (*cf.* Dt. 32:41–42).

12. Not only nature but also foreign *nations* will feel the presence of the Divine Warrior. As these Gentiles felt God's might during the Exodus and Conquest (*cf.* Dt. 4:38; 7:1; Ps. 9:5), so they will again (*cf.* Ps. 9:15–20; Is. 10:7). Among them will be the oppressor, Babylon (2:4–20; *cf.* Is. 13:4; 14:3–6). To accomplish this, God will 'stride' (JB) *through the earth*. This verb is used elsewhere of military marching (*cf.* 2 Sa. 5:24; 22:37), so continuing the warrior imagery (see vv. 8–9, 11). He will move in *wrath* (*cf.* v. 8), trampling them as a thresher threshes grain (1 Ch. 21:20; *cf.* Is. 25:10; Am. 1:3; Mi. 4:13).

13. In contrast to God's wrath upon Babylon, who threatens to overwhelm God's people, there is a promise of hope, of 'salvation' (RSV) for God's own covenant *people*. This term is specifically chosen as an indication of a special relationship with Yahweh not enjoyed by the Gentiles (*cf.* Ex. 3:7; Dt. 7:6; Ho. 1:9; 2:1). They are also called his *anointed* (Messiah), a term which usually refers to an individual. It could here be speaking of the king, one who is customarily anointed (*cf.* 1 Sa. 10:1; 16:12–13; 24:6, 10; 2 Sa. 12:7). He is the representative of the people (*cf.* Is. 7:8–9) and therefore his consecration by anointing would also be theirs.

The first half of the verse provides the key to understanding the relationship of this chapter to the rest of the book. Rather than ignoring wrongdoing (1:2–4), or allowing oppression of his people to go unpunished (1:12–17), God remembers his covenant and acts on their behalf. The whole purpose of the psalm and of God's theophany is to indicate the continued presence of gracious care coupled with divine judgment. Here we have God's answer to Habakkuk's complaints (1:12–17) – his people will be saved.

Military conquest of Babylon, the wicked, is resumed, using the imagery of 'striking the head'. This gesture is used idiomatically elsewhere to indicate a military defeat (Pss. 68:21; 110:5: *cf.* Nu. 24:17),[1] so again showing God as the warrior. This could also be an allusion to the 'head' being the ruler, the Babylonian king who would be struck and completely defeated (*cf.* 2 Sa. 22:39; Jb. 26:12; Pss. 18:38; 89:10). This contrasts the head which is struck in defeat with the head which is anointed in victory. God's enemy will be not only defeated but also completely *stripped* (3:9; see a similar action in 2:16), uncovered from head to toe as a sign of her humiliation (*cf.* Is. 47:3; La. 4:21; Ezk. 16:37).

14. The destruction of Israel's enemy will be a surprise to her, since the *warriors* (RSV, JB, NIV; 'leaders', NEB) of the wicked (v. 13) *stormed out* (*cf.* 1:9, 11) against God's people to rout and *to scatter* them like chaff (*cf.* Is. 24:1; 41:16; Je. 13:24; 18:17; Zp. 3:10). The enemy expected victory for herself and the chance to hide away and *devour* the plunder from her hapless victims like a carnivorous beast (*cf.* 1:8, 13; 2:5). The role of victor/victim is suddenly reversed under the power of God. Rather than triumphing, Babylon's *head*, or its 'leader' (JB; see v. 13), will be *pierced*, she will be defeated, and that by her *own spear* (lit. 'staff', v. 9; *cf.* v. 11 where another word for 'spear' is used), a possible reference to the fall of Babylonia to Cyrus without a fight.[2] The poor, those suffering oppression and hardship (*cf.* Ps. 10:2, 9; Is. 14:32; 54:11; Zp. 3:12), and the polar opposites of the wicked (v. 13), will receive the benefit of the mighty victory of God.

15. The section closes with the motif with which it opened in verse 8, God's *horses* trampling on the *sea*, an allusion to the crossing of the Red Sea (*cf.* Ex. 14:21–29; see the commentary on v. 8).

---

[1] See D. W. Baker, *Idiomatic Expressions in Hebrew and Akkadian Relating to the Head* (University of London, 1976), pp. 53–67, esp. pp. 54–56.
[2] See *ANET*, pp. 315–316.

D. Fear and faith (3:16-19a)

The person speaking changes again, this time with the prophet speaking in the first person of his own experiences (*cf.* introduction to vv. 8-15, p. 72). Habakkuk's questions are answered in such a way that he can pronounce one of the most powerful statements of faith recorded in Scripture.

16. The psalmist records his personal reactions of fear and awe at the power of the Warrior God (vv. 8-15). These are described in physiological terms (*cf.* Na. 2:10), with reactions being effected in the 'belly' (AV, NEB; *cf.* Gn. 25:23; Pr. 18:8; Ho. 12:3), *lips*, *bones* and the lower members (*legs*, NIV; 'feet', NEB). The first and last responses are expressed by the same word, *tremble*, which root has already occurred twice in the chapter (vv. 2, 7), though with different nuances.

The psalmist's response does not stop at fear. He has a sufficiently close relationship with God to be able to question him, and he also knows he can put his faith in him, trusting him to act responsibly. Therefore, relying upon the character of God, he can *wait* for him to act by moving against those *invading* Israel. This will take place on a calamitous *day* for Babylon, not the unique, eschatological 'Day of Yahweh' (see pp. 84-85), but a coming day of judgment reserved especially for them. This is shown by the lack of the Hebrew definite article, 'a day' rather than 'the day'. This, like similar days of judgment upon Israel and the nations, is but an anticipatory representation of what the final Day will be, a guarantee of its coming and an indication of its character as punishment for the wicked but joy for the followers of God. Babylon's day finally did come in 539 BC, when she fell to the Medes and Persians (see p. 45).

17-19a. The psalmist realizes that his faith can safely be put in Yahweh's grace, not only in matters of national survival but also of personal well-being and even existence. Judah had in the main an agrarian economy. She derived most of her sustenance from crops such as figs, grapes, olives and other produce of the fields, as well as livestock such as the flocks of sheep and goats and herds of cattle. Even though these sources might fail in some way, the psalmist sees that ultimately his existence is not based on them, but upon their source, Yahweh. He is the covenant *God* who keeps his promises, and in periods of affliction for his covenant people he is also their

Saviour (vv. 8, 13; *cf.* Ex. 15:1–2; 2 Sa. 22:3; Ps. 18:2, 46; Mi. 7:7). Even now, in the midst of doubt and oppression, the writer wants to rejoice (*cf.* Ps. 32:11; Is. 25:9; Joel 2:23). This is not because of any good on his own part, or because of any weakness on the part of his oppressors. His rejoicing is grounded in, and springs from, the relationship which God has with him and his people. Stripped of all else, he can never be deprived of his covenant God (*cf.* Jos. 1:5; Rom. 8:38–39). This is shown by the very word he uses to describe the saving God. Habakkuk, in the midst of deprivation and suffering, still feels able to call God 'mine' (*cf.* Ps. 63:1). The intimacy of the relationship is sure and solid, based as it is on the firm foundation of God's covenant promises of an eternal relationship with his people (*cf.* Dt. 7:6, 9) rather than being based on emotion or passing human whim (*cf.* Nu. 23:19; Ho. 11:9). This is a practical commentary on, and example of, the faith noted in 2:4.

Any strength or confidence which the psalmist possesses is due to the lordship of Yahweh and arises from him (*cf.* Ps. 18:32, 39; Joel 2:25). Not only does he provide stamina to endure hardship, God also provides vitality to walk on *heights* like a *deer* (*cf.* 2 Sa. 22:34; Ps. 18:33). The lighthearted prancing and gambolling of these creatures could reflect the skipping joy of the psalmist (*cf.* Jb. 21:11–12; Ec.3:4; Mt. 11:17). Assistance on the heights is found elsewhere (Dt. 32:13), although with a different verb, in the context of the conquest of the land and joyful possession of it (*cf.* Dt. 33:29). If this is the referent here, the entire chapter is united by its implicit and explicit references to the historical complex of Exodus-Sinai-Conquest. Habakkuk, who starts in depression, and doubt as to God's righteousness and justice, ends with a lively confidence in God's provision and sustaining power.

ZEPHANIAH

INTRODUCTION

I. THE TIMES AND PEOPLES

JOSIAH (640–609 BC) was the sixteenth king of Judah (2 Ki. 21:26 – 23:30; 2 Ch. 33:25 – 35:27), the southern kingdom which remained in the land after the exile of Israel in the north in 722 BC.[1] The prophecies under the name of Zephaniah are placed in his reign (1:1), and this dating has not been seriously disputed.[2] The prophet would thus have been a contemporary of Nahum, Habakkuk and Jeremiah. There has been discussion, however, as to when during the reign of this king the prophecies might have been given. Hezekiah, Josiah's great-grandfather, had restored Yahwistic worship, which had fallen into disfavour, to be replaced by idolatry and pagan practices (see 2 Ki. 18:4–6). The reform was short-lived, however, because his son, Manasseh, brought these forbidden practices back in a big way (2 Ki. 21:1–18) and Manasseh's son, Amon (2 Ki. 21:19–26), did nothing to redress the situation. It was only in the course of Josiah's reign (c. 621 BC) that Yahwism was again officially restored and the pagan practices proscribed. It could be argued that in the light of this proscription and the evidence in 1:4–9 of continued pagan influence the prophecies must have predated Josiah's reform. This is possible, but not certain, since official policy was not always and everywhere evidenced in public practice, even among the rulers of the nation. While the misdeeds in chapter 1 could reflect a pre-reform situation, they could instead be uneradicated syncretistic vestiges from after the reform had started.

The contemporaneity of this prophecy with at least the start

[1] *Cf.* J. Bright, *A History of Israel* (SCM Press/Westminster, ³1981), pp. 316–325.

[2] L. P. Smith and E. R. Lacheman, 'The authorship of the book of Zephaniah', *JNES* 9 (1950), pp. 137–142, proposed a date of *c.* 200 BC for this pseudepigraphical work, but their suggestion has not been well received.

81

of Jeremiah's ministry is supported by the latter's condemnation of some of the same pagan influences (Zp. 1:4–5; *cf.* Je. 2:8; 8:2; 19:5, 13; 32:35). The existence of these practices, which still needed condemnation by Jeremiah even after Zephaniah's ministry, would support the suggestion that Josiah's reform was not so radical and universal as might appear from Kings and Chronicles.

A detailed historical analysis of the events of Josiah's reign has argued for a setting of at least chapters 2 – 3 within the last decade before Josiah's reform.[1] This is based mainly on the picture of the historical interactions between Judah and the nations noted in 2:4–15. During this period Josiah was seeking to strengthen Judah, and to expand his sovereignty over surrounding territories as well (*cf.* 2 Ki. 23:15–20, where as part of his reforms he was able to exercise control of the neighbouring territory of Samaria).

The Philistines had been long-standing opponents of the Israelites from the time of the Conquest. They increased in power until the early monarchy, when David subdued them, though he was not able to eradicate their menace.[2] Philistia centred on five city-states adjacent to the Mediterranean. They were Ashdod, Ashkelon, Ekron, Gaza and Gath. The latter had faded to insignificance by Zephaniah's time, but the other four endured. They received warnings of judgment in the first oracle against the nations (2:4–7; *cf.* Is. 14:28–32; Je. 47; Am. 1:6–8; Zc. 9:5–7). The oracle of Zephaniah could well reflect the expansionist desires of Josiah. During his reign there is extra-biblical evidence of Judaean control of at least part of Philistia.[3]

Moab and Ammon, two Transjordanian neighbours of Israel, are ethnically linked according to the biblical record (Gn. 19:36–38). They also actively opposed Israel at times (*cf.* Nu. 22 – 24; Jos. 24:9; Jdg. 3:12–30; 11:17; 1 Sa. 11:1–11; 12:12; 14:47; 2 Ki. 1:1; 3:4–27; 2 Ch. 20:1–30), and would also have been naturally subject to Josiah's expansionary ideas due to their geographical proximity (2:8–11).[4]

Cush, or Ethiopia, had reached the zenith of its power when

[1] D. L. Christensen, 'Zephaniah 2:4–15: A Theological Basis for Josiah's Program of Political Expansion', *CBQ* (1984), pp. 669–682.
[2] See *POTT*, pp. 53–78; *NBD*, pp. 931–933.
[3] See the note of a Judaean governor in the area in *ANET*, p. 568.
[4] See *POTT*, pp. 229–258; *NBD*, pp. 30–31, 786–787.

it controlled Egypt in the Twenty-fifth Dynasty (*c.* 716–663 BC). It was ended in 663 BC by the Assyrian invasion of Egypt.[1] The destruction noted by Zephaniah (2:12) could be harking back to this event,[2] or the geographical designation could be used more loosely to mean Egypt as a whole (*cf.* Is. 20:4; Ezk. 30:4–9). As one of the two major powers in the area, it too faces the power of Israel's God, Yahweh (2:12; *cf.* 3:10).

Assyria was the other major nation during the eighth to seventh centuries BC.[3] It had defeated Israel in 722 BC, exiling the leaders of the country (*cf.* 2 Ki. 17:4–41; 18:9–12), and in the time of Josiah seemed invincible. By 612 BC, however, her capital, Nineveh (2:13), would be taken and the entire empire would have fallen by 605 BC to the Babylonians. The prophecy in Zephaniah (2:13–15) must therefore have been written some time prior to 612 BC.

The prophecy is directed in the first instance against Judah (1:4; *cf.* 1:1), and more specifically its capital city, Jerusalem (1:4, 12; 3:14, 16). The latter is also called Zion (3:14, 16), recalling the capture of the Jebusite city by David (*cf.* 2 Sa. 5:6–10; 1 Ki. 8:1). It is also known as God's holy city (*cf.* Ps. 48:1–2; Joel 3:16–17). Its sin means it does not deserve this connotation (1:4–9), but by Yahweh's grace her special status will be restored and she will again be able to bear this name (3:14–17).

II. THE MAN

Nothing much is known about the prophet Zephaniah apart from the brief biographical sketch found in the first verse of his prophecy. In this, the longest prophetic genealogy, he is descended from Hezekiah. This apparently refers to the fourteenth king of Judah (716-686 BC), who was also an ancestor of King Josiah, during whose reign Zephaniah prophesied (1:1). His name, 'Yahweh has hidden/protected', could be an indication of divine favour on a child born during the bloody and dangerous reign of Manasseh (686–642 BC; *cf.* 2 Ki. 21:16; 24:3–4).

Zephaniah's knowledge of the geography and demography

---

[1] Bright, *History of Israel*, p. 311; E. Ullendorff, *Ethiopia and the Bible* (Schweich Lectures; Oxford University Press, 1968); K. A. Kitchen, 'Cush', *NBD*, pp. 256–257.

[2] See Christensen, 'Theological Basis', p. 681.

[3] See *POTT*, pp. 156–178; *NBD*, pp. 98–103.

of Jerusalem (1:10–13; 3:1–4) implies that he was a long-time resident, if not a native, of the capital city. The prophet's interest in things priestly and sacrificial (1:4–5, 7–9; 3:4, 18) has suggested to some scholars that he was a prophet officially associated with the Temple, but the argument is not compelling. All committed Yahwists, especially one called by God as a prophet to his people, would be attracted to and concerned for the Temple as the earthly abode of their heavenly king. This interest, therefore, does not prove what is claimed for it, and would be much more remarkable if it were absent.

III. THE MESSAGE

The centre of Zephaniah's prophecies – uniting the book not only structurally (see the Analysis, p. 89) but theologically – is the concept of the Day of Yahweh. While not the first (*cf.* Am. 5:18–20; 8:9–14; Is. 2; 13; 34; Joel 2) nor the last (*cf.* Je. 46 – 51; Ezk. 7) of the prophets to write on this subject, such devotion to a single theme is not found in any other.

The fact that this day is like a two-sided coin, comprising two separate yet related facets, is more fully developed here than in other prophets, where usually one element is stressed to the deprivation or exclusion of the other. The two facets of the same Day of the Lord are judgment and blessing. The day is characterized by both; each affects the same people and occupies a similar time-frame, but each has a different cause.

The announcement of God's impending judgment on mankind in general (1:2–3), and on his people Judah in particular (1:4–6), leads to a consideration of that aspect of the Day of the Lord (1:8–18; 2:4 – 3:8). This day is near (1:7, 14) – near and getting rapidly nearer. It is being precipitated by the sins of Yahweh's covenant people, Israel, as well as the wrongs of mankind at large. The former involve repeated and fundamental breaches of the covenant promises on the part of the population as a whole (1:4–6, 12) as well as the leaders (3:3–4). These sins include syncretistic elements (1:4–5), in breach of the first commandment (Ex. 20:3; Dt. 5:7). Also prevalent is apathy, an attitude that reasoned, 'If the covenant-making God is no longer interested in the people, then why should they respond to him in obedience?' (1:12). This is coupled with pride, assurance of one's own self-sufficiency (*cf.* 2:3).

The sins of the nations also contribute to their judgment at God's hand (*cf.* Gn. 6:5–7; Am. 1:3 – 2:3). While not every nation mentioned is charged with specific wrongs, there are two identified which correspond to the sins condemned in Judah. Moab's insults and threats against God's people (2:8) were an insult to Yahweh himself as their king. The lack of interest shown by his own people in himself and his potency (1:12) led the neighbouring nations to have the same attitude. They felt that God could be blatantly despised with impunity. This is coupled with their own pride (2:10; *cf.* v. 15), self-assurance in their own devices which corresponds to that of Judah itself.

Because of this universal provocation, Yahweh will be moved to universal judgment. The sovereign of all the earth will exercise his sovereignty globally and punish all who oppose him. God's response is not at all capricious and gratuitous, however, but is exactly that, a response based on his character as a just and holy God who, being himself bound by covenant, also holds others to their covenant obligations. This judgment, while universal, is not permanent, since there is still another facet to the Day of the Lord.

The second aspect of the day involves blessing. This is not the result of any external impulse, but rather rises from Yahweh's character as a covenant-keeping God. He offers hope to his own people (3:11–20), not only because some will return to the covenant (*cf.* Dt. 30, esp. v. 2), but also because he has never left it; his promises will be kept. Those who will be blessed are the remnant (2:3, 9; 3:12–13), those who humbly trst in him as able to do good, rather than relying on their own pride (*cf.* 1:12; 2:3). Hope is also extended to the nations (3:9–10). Although they were not beneficiaries of the Mosaic covenant, they are the recipients of Yahweh's grace.

Both facets of the Day of Yahweh share two time-frames. The immediate message to Judah is that she and the nations will be punished in the very near future (1:4–18), but that hope is also a possibility in the short term (2:3). The message is expanded, however, in that both aspects leave the realm of historical proximity and move towards eschatological fulfilment. In the unspecified future both Judah and the nations will face not only judgment (3:11, 8 respectively), but also enjoy benefit (3:13–17, 9 respectively).

Another important aspect of the prophecy arises when one

notices the serious moral and spiritual decline following the vigorous reforms of Hezekiah (see p. 81), which would in turn follow those being undertaken by Zephaniah's contemporary Josiah (see 2 Ki. 23:31 – 24:4). Dependence on the faith and piety of a preceding generation is not enough. A personal commitment to the covenant was needed by each successive king and each generation of Israel, as it still is for each generation in the church. Neither the twentieth-century church nor the Israel of the monarchy can be second-generation children of God. The commitment must be made individually and personally by everyone.

IV. THE BOOK

The integrity of the book has been questioned, but there is no objective evidence that Zephaniah was circulated in any other than its present form. The only editorial note in the book is the heading, and it is not possible to be certain when such a note was added to the collection of oracles. The most logical time for additions would be when the collection itself was made, which could just as well have been during the later years of the prophet's life as any subsequent period.

Various scholars have proposed secondary additions to the book and have generally based these proposals on two different grounds. Firstly, there are those passages which could represent a historical period after the reign of Josiah, during which the book claims to be placed. For example, 2:15 paints Nineveh as having been destroyed, and so presupposes its fall in 612 BC. A common form in Hebrew prophecy, however, is the 'prophetic perfect', a verb form indicating a completed action. When God made a statement of future intent or of prediction, the Hebrew prophets saw these events as being sure and as good as accomplished, due to the sovereignty and power of their source, so they were often described as already accomplished. Secondly, a proposal has been made that in the pre-exilic period the prophetic message was one of judgment, meeting the people at their point of need – repentance from sin. During the exile, however, the need had altered. People suffering exile and questioning the faithfulness or even the presence of Yahweh required not a message of judgment, but rather one of hope. Therefore, passages of hope must be exilic (3:9–20). The argument, however, is circular and based on presuppositions rather than evidence. The only objective evidence is the canonical text in which both judgment and hope are mixed, sometimes in different proportions, but with both present nevertheless. If one comes with one's hypothesis and emends the text to fit it, one is not treating the evidence with integrity.

The logical unity of the book can be seen in its contents (see p. 89): judgment (1:2–6) leads the prophet to think of the ultimate judgment, the Day of Yahweh (1:7 – 3:20), which is portrayed in both of its aspects. That day does involve judgment for those not abiding by God's covenant (1:8 – 3:8), but it also involves hope through God's grace (3:9–20).

The prophecy, though a unity, is composed of smaller units marked by changes in addressee, content, literary form, *etc.* Literary genres used include judgment oracles (1:2–3, 4–6, 8–9, *etc.*), calls for response (1:7; 2:1–3; 3:8) – including a call to praise and a psalm of praise (3:14–17) – as well as salvation oracles (3:9–13, 18–20). The individual units evidence internal integrity, as shown in particular in the psalm of joy (3:14–17). Its literary structure is that of concentric parallelism, in which the first element corresponds to the last, the second to the next-to-last, and so on, with the climax, 'no more fear', in the centre. Here the rejoicing of the people on account of God's love, at the beginning of the psalm, corresponds to Yahweh's joy over their return to him at the psalm's conclusion. God, the mighty actor, and his presence so surround the climactic message of hope to Jerusalem, the city of God, that they are not to fear. This can be seen in the following diagram:

A	Zion singing (3:14a)
B	Israel's shouts (3:14b)
C	Jerusalem's joy (3:14c)
D	Yahweh's deliverance (3:15a, b)
E	Presence of Yahweh the king (3:15c)
F	No more fear (3:15d)
G	Jerusalem's future message (3:16a)
F¹	No more fear (3:16b, c)
E¹	Presence of Yahweh the God (3:17a)
D¹	The mighty deliverer (3:17b)
C¹	God's joy (3:17c)
B¹	Yahweh's silence (3:17d)
A¹	Yahweh singing (3:17e)

The last two verses of the prophecy are also united by the repetition of a form of step or synthetic parallelism. In both verses 19 and 20 the adverbial time indicator 'at that time' helps open the first element, which has as its main component the gathering of God's people. The next two elements involve the bestowal of 'praise and honour', which will take place world-wide ('in every land', v. 19; 'all the peoples', v. 20). This parallelism can be diagrammed as:

<pre>
A   At that time – gathering
  B   Praise and honour
    C   In every land
A¹   At that time – gathering
  B¹   Praise and honour
    C¹   Among all peoples
</pre>

The whole message of Zephaniah is finally united in one grand inclusio,[1] in that it begins and ends with Yahweh, Israel's just but caring covenant God, whose word (1:1) is spoken (3:20).

---

[1] A repetition of key elements, whether words or motifs, at the beginning and end of a literary unit.

ANALYSIS

I. HEADING (1:1)

II. JUDGMENT (1:2–6)
A. Mankind (1:2–3)
B. Judah and Jerusalem (1:4–6)

III. THE DAY OF YAHWEH (1:7 – 3:20)
A. Announcement (1:7)
B. The nature of the day – judgment (1:8–18)
  i. Judgment of God's people (1:8–13)
  ii. Judgment of the world (1:14–18)
C. The required response (2:1–3)
D. Specific scenarios of judgment (2:4 – 3:8)
   i. Philistia (2:4–7)
  ii. Moab and Ammon (2:8–11)
  iii. Cush (2:12)
  iv. Assyria (2:13–15)
  v. Jerusalem (3:1–7)
     a. Sins compounded (3:1–5)
     b. Demonstration ignored (3:6–7)
  vi. The world (3:8)
E. The nature of the day – hope (3:9–20)
  i. Nations converted (3:9–10)
  ii. The remnant preserved (3:11–13)
  iii. A psalm of joy (3:14–17)
  iv. God's promise (3:18–20)

COMMENTARY

I. HEADING (1:1)

The book is given a very general designation as *the word of the Lord* (*cf.* Je. 1:2; Ezk. 1:3; Ho. 1:1; Joel 1:1; Jon. 1:1; Mi. 1:1; Hg. 1:1; Zc. 1:1; Mal. 1:1), indicating its source as being the covenant God of Israel (*cf.* Ex. 6:2–6). The recipient of the message is *Zephaniah*, who is further identified, in the longest genealogy of any prophet (*cf.* Je. 36:14), by apparently being a descendant of *Hezekiah*, the fourteenth king of Judah (716–686 BC; *cf.* 2 Ki. 18:1–20:21; see p. 81). The genealogy could have stretched this far to indicate that the writer was an Israelite rather than an Ethiopian, as one could translate the name of his father, *Cushi* (*cf.* Gn. 10:6; 2 Ki. 19:9; Is. 18:1). His nationality is clear, however, since all of the other names in the genealogy, including the prophet's own, contain a form of the name of Israel's God, Yah(weh). The lack of designation of Hezekiah (a common name in Israel, *cf.* 1 Ch. 3:13; Ezr. 2:16; Ne. 7:21; 10:17) as 'king of Judah' does not disallow this interpretation, since the phrase is used elsewhere in the verse to identify *Josiah*, the seventeenth king of Judah (640–609 BC; *cf.* 2 Ki. 22:1 – 23:30; see pp. 81–82). It could have been used only once in order to avoid duplication.

II. JUDGMENT (1:2–6)

God's first words are judgment, initially directed towards all animate creatures (vv. 2–3), and then narrowing down to his own people, Judah, and more specifically the inhabitants of Jerusalem (vv. 4–6). Not only are those to be punished identified, but also some of their sins are indicated. Yahweh presents himself as being personally involved in his judgment, which will be devastating in its totality.

A. Mankind (1:2–3)

These two verses are united by the concept of 'sweeping away', which occurs four times in the Hebrew, showing the emphatic and comprehensive nature of the action (*cf.* Est. 9:28; Ps. 73:19; Je. 8:13).[1] This emphasis is reinforced by the objects of the verbs; *everything*, *men* and *animals*, including *birds* and *fish*, will be done away with. This judgment by God will be the undoing of his creation, as all of these words are found in Genesis (1:20, 24, 25, 26–28). The whole *face of the earth* (*cf.* Gn. 2:6; Je. 28:16) will be swept clean. Mankind is singled out in a particular way since it is he who will be *cut off*, a strong word indicating annihilation (1:4; *cf.* Lv. 26:22; 1 Ki. 9:7; 11:16; Ezk. 14:13). It is used at times in the technical sense of carrying out the death penalty (*cf.* Ex. 31:14; Lv. 20:3–6).

The severity of the statements and the certainty of their realization are emphasized by twice affirming that these are declarations of Yahweh, *declares the Lord*.

B. Judah and Jerusalem (1:4–6)

4. While the whole of animate creation will be destroyed (1:2–7), *Judah* and her capital and major city *Jerusalem* are given special mention, since they are the people of God. All are guilty, but God's people more so, since they had voluntarily entered into a covenant relationship with Yahweh (*cf.* Am. 1:3 – 2:16, where nations are judged, but Judah and Israel more severely). In a gesture of chastisement and judgment, God will *stretch out* his *hand against* Israel (*cf.* 2:13; Is. 5:25; Je. 51:25; Ezk. 16:27; 25:7).

The record of those to be *cut off*, punished because of their sins, is connected to the description of universal destruction by an exact repetition of the verb form (*cf.* v. 3). They will be removed *from this place*, referring at least to Jerusalem, and possibly more specifically to the Temple, which is 'the Place' *par excellence* (*cf.* Dt. 12:5, 11; 1 Ki. 8:29, 30; Ezk. 42:13).

The remainder of these three verses contains a list of those to be destroyed. The *remnant of Baal* is those who still worship this foreign god. Usually the word, literally 'master, owner',

---

[1] The first Hebrew form could be repointed to indicate that the action was being repeated, done again, a reference to Gn. 8:21, though there is no manuscript evidence for the change.

refers to the Canaanite god Hadad,[1] whose worship was a longstanding snare to Israel (*cf.* Jdg. 6:25; 1 Ki. 16:31–32; 18). During this period of the prophet's life, Judah was under the control of Assyria, who also had a deity named Bel (Baal) and used the word as referring to a god.[2] This could then refer to Mesopotamian syncretism, which would be expected during this period of their domination. It has been suggested that the presence of continued Baal-worship indicates a time for the prophecy prior to Josiah's reforms in 621 BC (see p. 81). Following the reform, it is argued, it would have disappeared. This date might be correct, but a reference to a *remnant of Baal* could indicate that most, though not all, vestiges of pagan religion had been extinguished. Even at the height of the reform not all traces of pagan influence were eradicated, however, since it sprang up again soon after Josiah's death (*cf.* 2 Ch. 36:13–14; Je. 9:13; 19:4–5; see p. 80).

Not only are foreign deities *cut off,* but also the very mention (*names*) of *pagan . . . priests*[3] is obliterated. The word is used only of non-Yahwistic priests (*cf.* 2 Ki. 23:5; Ho. 10:5). This rare form is explained by the regular Hebrew word for priest.

5. Worship of astral deities ('the host of the heavens', AV, RSV, *cf.* Dt. 4:19; 2 Ki. 17:16; 21:3, 5; Je. 8:2) was performed *on the roofs* (Je. 19:13; *cf.* 32:29). These were also deities worshipped both by the Canaanites and the Assyrians (*cf.* the zodiac), so either could be referred to here.

Syncretistic religious practices are doomed too. More Yahweh worshippers who *swear by* him also do the same by 'their king' (NJB mg., MT). Some revocalize this, following an LXX recension, to read 'Milcom', an Ammonite god (*cf.* 1 Ki. 11:5, 33; 2 Ki. 23:13), while the existing form also corresponds to a Babylonian deity.[4] However interpreted, what is strongly condemned is mixing worship of the true, covenant God of Israel with that of another deity (*cf.* Ex. 20:3; Dt. 5:7). Swearing by another god meant acknowledging his authority, something which was denied to Israel.

6. The misdeeds are summarized and encapsulated by lastly

---

[1] See *IBD*, p. 153 and references there.

[2] See the article on *belu* in I. J. Gelb *et al.* (eds.), *The Assyrian Dictionary*, 2 (Oriental Institute, 1965), p. 193.

[3] *kōmer*, possibly a loan word from the cognate Akkadian *kumru*, 'priest' (see *ibid.*, 8 (1971), pp. 534–535).

[4] See the article on *malku*, B, *ibid*, 10 (1977), pp. 168–169.

noting *those who turn back*, become apostate (*cf.* Pss. 53:3; 78:57; Is. 59:13) and no longer follow after Yahweh, nor *seek* (2:3; *cf.* Pss. 27:8; 105:4; Ho. 5:6) him as their God, nor 'consult him' (NEB; *cf.* 2 Ki. 22:13; Ps. 105:4; Is. 55:6; Am. 5:6) for guidance and hope. There is in these verses, therefore, a range of religious response – from the desired total commitment to Yahweh alone, through a syncretistic mixture of Yahwistic and pagan worship, to absolute paganism and practical atheism towards Yahweh, who is completely abandoned. The people were to have kept themselves from all of these paganizing practices and remained a holy people to Yahweh alone, but since they have failed to do so, God himself will effect their purification.

III. THE DAY OF YAHWEH (1:7 – 3:20)

The multi-faceted nature of the Day of Yahweh (see pp. 84–85) is presented in the rest of the book. It is a day of judgment (1:8 – 3:8) and a day of hope (3:9–20). It is a day specifically relevant to God and his covenant people (1:8–13; 2:1–3; 3:1–7), but also of significance for other nations (1:14–18; 2:4–15). It is a day of historical fulfilment (2:4–15), but also of eschatological and apocalyptic expectation (1:14–18; 3:8–13). It is the day when Yahweh will act in all of his justice and righteousness, judgment and loving mercy; he alone is at the centre of the stage, and therefore it is his day.

A. Announcement (1:7)

In the presence of the 'Lord Yahweh' (JB; *Sovereign Lord*, NIV), the ruler and supreme God (*cf.* Dt. 10:17; Jos. 3:13), the hearers are commanded to *be silent*, an interjection of awe and respect used mainly in the prophets (*cf.* Am. 6:10; 8:3; Hab. 2:20; Zc. 2:13, but see also Jdg. 3:19). In this case, Yahweh's presence is evident in the nearness (*cf.* v. 14; Is. 13:6; Ezk. 7:7; 30:3; Joel 1:15; 2:1; 3:14; Ob. 15) of the Day of Yahweh. Not only is it *near*, but Yahweh has made the necessary preparations for it. He has 'readied' a *sacrifice* or sacrificial feast, an event at times associated with judgment (*cf.* Is. 34:6; Je. 46:10; Ezk. 39:17–20). Those who are 'called' or *invited* by Yahweh ('guests', RSV, NEB, JB) to participate in the feast are *consecrated* or set apart for a specific function (*cf.* Ex. 28:41; Lv. 21:8; 2 Sa. 8:11; Is. 13:3). The irony here is that it is apparently the guests invited to the sacrificial celebrations who are themselves going to serve as the sacrifice (*cf.* Gn. 22, esp. vv. 7, 9). A sacrifice to please Yahweh is made by the offering up to his judgment of those who displeased him.

B. The nature of the day – judgment (1:8–18)

The most immediate experience that Israel and the nations would have of the Day of Yahweh is as a day of judgment. Firstly, additional specific faults of God's people are enumerated for punishment, centring mainly on Jerusalem and the religious and economic practices carried on there (vv. 8–13). Then the nature of the day and its consequences for all of mankind are detailed (vv. 14–18), though recapitulation of some motifs binds the two sections together.

i. Judgment of God's people (1:8–13). 8. A new section opens with a time reference 'and it will be'. This passage is directly related to the previous one, however, since it describes some of the things which will happen at the *day of . . . sacrifice* (*cf.* v. 7), combining the two previously separate but related motifs of the Day of Yahweh and of sacrifice. The first stage is the punishment (*cf.* vv. 9, 12; 3:7) of the 'officers' and 'princes'. Exactly who these people are is a matter of debate. If the prophecy took place early in Josiah's reign (see v. 4 and p. 82), these officials could have been men who exercised authority during his minority (*cf.* 2 Ki. 22:1), who were not as devoted to Yahweh as they should have been. The princes could be those of the royal line who, apart from the godly Josiah himself, were also lacking in piety. Exactly who is specifically intended, the civil leadership in general has failed in its duties and is under divine condemnation.

Another, apparently numerous, group under judgment includes those who were wearing *foreign clothes*. These could have been wearing special garments used for pagan religious practices (*cf.* 2 Ki. 10:22), since the adjective is associated with pagan deities (*cf.* Mal. 2:11). At the least the threat indicates an abhorrence of foreign influences which too often led to the syncretism already condemned (1:4–6; *cf.* 1

Ki. 11:1–8; Ne. 13:30).

9. A third group of miscreants are those who 'leap' (RSV) like a hart (*cf.* Is. 35:6) 'over' (or *on*) the *threshold*, a word always associated with a temple (*cf.* 1 Sa. 5:4–5; Ezk. 9:3; 10:4, 18; 46:2; 47:1). The problem in interpreting this obscure passage is that the last word is not clearly enough understood, and therefore neither is the practice, although the context suggests that it too is probably a pagan ritual. It could refer to the Philistine practice of not stepping on the 'threshold' of Dagon's temple (1 Sa. 5:4–5) having been adopted in Israel, but there is no compelling evidence in favour of it. Another explanation of what will happen *on that day* is possible if one sees the second clause of the verse as explaining the obscure first clause. This is grammatically possible, and would result not in a religious but a social wrong. These people 'fill the house of their lords' with *violence* (*cf.* Gn. 6:11; Hab. 1:2–3, 9) and *deceit*. This could refer to their royal palaces which are filled and ready to overflow in violence (*cf.* Am. 3:10) instead of the justice and righteousness which is expected of a king. More probably in this context of religious wrongdoing, the 'lords' referred to could be the pagan gods, a term used to describe them elsewhere.[1] This is in contradistinction and direct opposition to Yahweh, the true Lord (v. 7). Their worship is fraudulent and violent, not containing truth or hope or peace.

10–11. Continuing his solemn statement (see vv. 2–3) concerning *that day* (see vv. 7, 8, 9) of sacrifice, the prophet describes the responses of the inhabitants of Jerusalem's districts and environs. They will *cry* in distress (*cf.* Gn. 27:34; Ps. 9:12; Je. 48:3) and *wail* (v. 11; *cf.* Is. 15:8; Je. 25:36; Zc. 11:3) at the destruction and judgment which will take place (see v. 13). The third response is literally 'a great breaking', usually interpreted as the crashing uproar accompanying destruction, as in the English versions. It is also, however, used in the context of anguished cries (*cf.* Is. 15:5; 65:14; Je. 48:5; 51:54), a usage which fits well in this context.

Specific geographical locations in Jerusalem are noted as places where these cries originated. The *Fish Gate* was on the

---

[1] See C.-F. Jean and J. Hoftijzer, *Dictionnaire des inscriptions sémitiques de l'ouest* (E. J. Brill, 1965), p. 5.

north of the city (*cf.* 2 Ch. 33:14; Ne. 3:3; 12:39), probably the main gate there.[1] Due to the steep slopes on the other sides of Jerusalem, the city was most vulnerable from the north. The 'Second' (AV, RSV, NEB) or *New Quarter* (NJB, NIV) was, according to its name, a more recent addition, lying to the north of the Temple and the main part of the city (*cf.* 2 Ki. 22:14; possibly Ne. 11:9).[2] *The hills* are a more general description, although at the time they could well have had a more specific, locally known reference. Since the previous two locations lay in northern Jerusalem, these hills could well have been there as well.

The same theme of impending distress is continued, though now people are commanded to *wail* as the time of doom has now arrived. Those addressed are those who inhabit the 'Mortar' (RSV, JB, NIV mg.), possibly a quarry hollowed out to resemble a mortar (*cf.* Jdg. 15:19; Pr. 27:22). Due to the progression of movement through the previous locations, this region probably lies south of the Second Quarter. The following context suggests that it is a *market* area (*cf.* 'the street of the bakers' in Je. 37:21). The cause of anguish is the destruction (*cf.* 2 Sa. 21:5; Ho. 4:6; Ob. 5) or 'wiping out' (NEB, JB; 'cut off', AV, RSV) of those who deal in *silver*, either bankers or merchants themselves. In a parallel statement, these are called the 'people of Canaan', a nation whose trading expertise thrived through later centuries when they were known as the Phoenicians, and whose mercantile operations of even earlier appear to be proverbial (*cf.* Jb. 41:6; Pr. 31:24; Is. 23:8; Ezk. 16:29; Ho. 12:7). Not only pagan religious practices but also business, in particular its foreign influences (*cf.* 1 Ki. 5:11; 9:26–28), will be brought down. No reason for this commercial collapse is given here, but dishonest practice probably played a major role, as it did for other prophets (Am. 8:5–6; Mi. 6:10–11). God is therefore concerned not only with religious perversion but also with economic misconduct.

12–13. Yahweh then turns his attention *at that time* (*cf.* v. 7, 8, 9, 10) to *Jerusalem* in its entirety, culminating in his entry from the north into the city (vv. 10–11). He will *search* there *with lamps* so that none may escape (*cf.* 1 Ki. 20:6; 2 Ki. 10:23;

[1] See a possible location in Y. Aharoni and M. Avi-Yonah, *The Macmillan Bible Atlas* (Macmillan, 1968), map 170.
[2] *Ibid.*, map 114.

Lk. 15:8). Unlike Diogenes, the pre-Christian Greek philosopher who was searching for an honest man, Yahweh in this context does not seek righteousness but sin to *punish* and eradicate (*cf.* Is. 10:12; Je. 6:15; 44:13). In this case the sin is not of commission (*cf.* vv. 4–11) but of omission. The men[1] who will be punished are described by using a metaphor which draws on part of the fermentation process of *wine*. When wine sits quietly, the heavier solid particles settle, leaving the dregs at the bottom of the cask or bottle. This can lead to thickening or coagulation if the wine is left too long (*cf.* Ex. 15:8; Jb. 10:10). Rather than being of use, like fine aged wine (*cf.* Is. 25:6), the rich and influential of Jerusalem, those with *wealth* (NEB, JB, NIV), *houses*, *vineyards* and *wine*, will stagnate in indifference and quietism. G. A. Smith clearly expressed the problem when he wrote: 'The great causes of God and Humanity are not defeated by the hot assaults of the Devil, but by the slow, crushing, glacier-like mass of thousands and thousands of indifferent nobodies. God's causes are never destroyed by being blown up, but by being sat upon.'[2]

Rather than condemning the use of alcohol, as the passage could be understood (NEB), Zephaniah condemns apathy. This is exacerbated by the practical atheism of the people. While not necessarily denying the existence of Yahweh on a theoretical level, they deny his activity on a pragmatic level, either for *good* or *bad*. Blessing or grief do not issue from him.

This view of the non-involvement of God in national life is a serious heresy for Israel, flying in the face of the Israelite view of God as continually and actively involved in history, from the creation through the call of Abram, the Exodus, his meeting with Israel at Sinai, the Conquest, and his constant attention to the affairs of the Israelite state. The lack of an actual, historical intervention of God in the events of the world for both blessing and punishment would render their faith as meaningless as the Christian faith would be if Jesus had not

---

[1] A suggested textual emendation involving moving one letter and duplicating another results in 'those who are at ease' (see NIV; *cf.* Is. 32:9, 11; Am. 6:1; Zc. 1:15). Complacency and false security exactly fit the context as interpreted for this verse, but lack of manuscript evidence for the proposed reading tells against it.

[2] G. A. Smith, p. 54.

actually, historically risen from the dead.[1]

Zephaniah shows that this irresponsible theology is just as evil as an outright revolt against God. It will issue in the destruction and confiscation of the very sources of the power belonging to those who refuse to stir themselves to use it for good (*cf.* Dt. 28:30–42; Am. 5:11; Mi. 6:15).

ii. Judgment of the world (1:14–18). Zephaniah now turns to a description of the Day of Yahweh (see v. 7), with its cataclysmic battles which will affect the entire world and from which wealth will not be a protection. The focus of the prophecy thus moves from a nationalistic message to Judah to a universal, eschatological warning to all people.

The concept of the day has moved from a naive, popular understanding of it as involving only Yahweh's final elevation of his people to global supremacy simply because they were chosen by him (see Am. 5:18–20). Election also implies responsibility (Am. 3:2), so the Day of Yahweh in the prophets also shows the aspect of judgment if responsibility is ignored. Also, the day is not only of national import, but is shown here to affect all nations. This development of the two-sided nature (see pp. 84–85) and the universality of the eschatological day culminates in Christ's second coming, the final day (*cf.* 2 Thes. 2:2), which is both two-sided and universal (*cf.* Mt. 24:3–33; 1 Cor. 5:5; Rev. 19 – 22).

14. An important aspect of the Day of Yahweh (*cf.* Is. 2:6–22; Joel 2:1–11; Am. 5:18–20) for the prophet is that it is *near* in time (see v. 7), something which is emphasized here by repetition and the emphatic position of the word at the start of the Hebrew verse. It is near, and rapidly getting nearer.[2] The day is also *great* (*cf.* Joel 2:11, 31; Mal. 4:5) in its importance for all of creation.

The description of some of the characteristics of the day

---

[1] See the classic presentation of the importance of historical reality for a meaningful faith in L. B. Gilkey, 'Cosmology, Ontology, and the Travail of Biblical Language', *JR* 41 (1961), pp. 194–205.

[2] The Hebrew adverbial form, 'hurrying', may be understood from extra-biblical Egyptian, Phoenician and Ugaritic sources to be some kind of soldier – a metaphor for Yahweh the Divine Warrior (see p. 72) – who is approaching, in synonymous parallelism with the coming day. See A. F. Rainey, 'The soldier-scribe in *Papyrus Anastasi* I', *JNES* 26 (1967), pp. 58–60.

continues through to verse 16, beginning here with an ambiguous term which could be a 'voice' (AV) which is *bitter*, but it is difficult to understand the Day of Yahweh possessing a voice. Others have seen this as a reference to the 'sound', 'noise' or 'din' of the day (RSV, JB). Possibly most satisfactory in the context would be an exclamation equivalent to 'hark'; a voice is audible (*cf.* Is. 40:3, 6) and its message involves not only bitterness but also a 'battle cry' given by a *warrior* (Is. 42:13; *cf.* Zp. 3:17).

15–16. A catalogue of frightful characteristics of *that day* (see v. 14) is given in staccato style, with the word 'day' repeated six times in these two verses, a possible echo of the six 'good' days of creation (Gn. 1:1–31).[1] It is brought to life as full of *wrath* on the part of Yahweh (*cf.* v. 18; Ezk. 7:19; Ho. 5:10; Hab. 3:8). Five synonymous word pairs describe its effects on man. The first involves emotional *distress* and *anguish* (see also RSV, and *cf.* NEB and JB; *cf.* v. 17; Gn. 35:3; Jb. 15:24; Ps. 25:17; Ob. 12, 14; Na. 1:7). The next involves physical 'destruction' (NEB) and 'devastation' (RSV, NEB, JB; *cf.* Jb. 30:3; 38:27; Ps. 35:8; Is. 47:11), a word play on two forms from the same Hebrew root.[2] Terror is enhanced by *darkness* (*cf.* Jb. 3:4; Joel 2:2; Am. 5:18, 20) and *gloom* (*cf.* Ex. 10:22; Is. 8:22; 58:10; Joel 2:2), *clouds* (*cf.* Ps. 97:2; Ezk. 30:3; 34:12; Joel 2:2) and *blackness* or 'deep darkness' (see RSV; *cf.* Is. 60:2; Je. 13:16; Ezk. 34:12). These manifestations, as well as 'trumpet blast' (RSV, *cf.* Is. 27:13; Ezk. 33:3; Am. 2:2) and *battle cry* (*cf.* Jos. 6:5; Jdg. 7:18, 22; Am. 1:14; 2:2), are characteristic of the tumult and terror of a theophany, when the all-powerful God met with his people (*cf.* Ex. 19:16–19; 20:18; Dt. 4:11). God the warrior is setting out in battle not only against the enemies of his people (see the commentary on 3:17) but also against his people as well, since they are acting at this stage as the enemies of God. In the case of Zephaniah's audience, the mighty presence of Yahweh on his day is not for blessing, as they experienced it at Mt Sinai, but for judgment. Even Judah's strongholds, whether *fortified* (*cf.* Nu. 13:28; Dt. 3:5; Is. 36:1; Ho. 8:14) or with 'lofty corner towers' (*cf.* 2 Ch. 26:15), will not be able to stand God's wrath.

The possible echo of Genesis 1 noted above could indicate that the judgment portrayed here is to be seen as a reversal

---

[1] See Craigie, p. 116.   [2] *shō'âh, meshô'âh.*

of creation. Man's sin leads to God's punishment, which in effect brings creation full-circle to where it was before God actively formed the universe. Light gives way to darkness, and the order of the well-established creation reverts to disorder (*cf.* Gn. 1:2; Je. 4:23–26). God's sovereign benevolence in his good provisions is replaced by judgment, and his blessings are withheld.

17–18. Yahweh, whose presence was powerfully felt in the description of his day (vv. 14–16), now speaks personally. He shows that judgment is not restricted to Judah alone but applies to all 'mankind' (*cf.* Gn. 1:26–27). Upon them Yahweh will *bring distress* (*cf.* v. 15; Dt. 28:57; 1 Ki. 8:37; Je. 10:18), so they will stagger and grope for direction like *blind* people, their blindness being a curse for wrongful deeds (*cf.* Dt. 28:28, 29; Is. 59:10; La. 4:14; Acts 9:8) in sinning 'against Yahweh' himself. This last clause is apparently a note by the prophet, since it talks about Yahweh rather than describing him as speaking. It serves as a transition between the first half of the verse, in which Yahweh is actively involved as the subject of the verb, and the last half of the verse, where the verbs are passive. Yahweh is still the one causing the actions, but he is not explicitly mentioned. As *dust* is cheap and of little value due to its quantity (*cf.* 2 Ki. 13:7; Is. 41:2; Zc. 9:3), so will be the shed *blood* of the sinners (*cf.* Gn. 9:6; Ps. 79:3). The verb does double duty, having a second object, which is as worthless as 'dung' (RSV, *cf.* 1 Ki. 14:10; Jb. 20:7; Ezk. 4:12, 15). The exact identity of this second, valueless object is unclear. The only other use of the word (Jb. 20:23) provides no help for the present context, and the English versions appear to derive their translations ('flesh', AV, RSV; 'corpses', JB; 'bowels', NEB; *entrails*, NIV) from the context. Another option which merits consideration is to read the revocalized word as 'sap', the life fluid which parallels 'blood' in the sentence.[1]

Mankind sought salvation from judgment in *silver* and *gold*, perhaps a reference to their riches (vv. 11, 13; *cf.* Je. 4:30), but more likely to idols which were commonly made from these materials (*cf.* Is. 2:20; 30:22; Ezk. 7:19–20). Natural objects or symbols of non-existent gods will not save on this day, again characterized by Yahweh's *wrath* (v. 15). His *jeal-*

---

[1] *lēaḥ* with enclitic *mem*; see Sabottka, p. 57; R. L. Smith, p. 128.

ousy, the fierce protection of God's unique position as sole creator and covenant God (see p. 27; *cf.* Ps. 79:5; Ezk. 16:38, 42; 36:5), 'devours' *the whole world* (see vv. 2–3; 2 Pet. 3: 10–12) as with *fire* (3:8; *cf.* Dt. 4:24). This last clause is repeated as a kind of refrain in 3:8 (see p. 114). Specifically it is the earth's 'inhabitants' (RSV) who will be completely and quickly brought to an *end* (*cf.* Is. 10:23; 28:22; Je. 30:11; Na. 1:8). God's punishment, like the sin which necessitated it, is thus both universal and radical.

C. The required response (2:1–3)

Attention is again turned to God's own people (see 1:4–13) after a broader look at universal judgment (1:14–18), which is resumed later (vv. 4–15). Harsh judgment is present still (v. 2), but now it could be tempered with hope if the correct response to Yahweh should be made (v. 3).

1–2. God's people are this time called a *nation* (*gôy*), the usual description of pagan people. Although at times used of Israel itself (*e.g.* Ex. 19:6; Dt. 4:6; Is. 1:4; 9:3; 10:6; *cf.* Zp. 2:9), the term could have been used deliberately to equate *shameful* ('shameless', RSV) Israel with the pagan nations in their behaviour and attitude towards God. They do not acknowledge him, though this is the prerequisite of truly being the covenant people (*'am*) of Yahweh (vv. 8–9; *cf.* Ex. 6:7; Dt. 7:6). They are called to *gather* themselves *together . . . before* it is too late. The description of the people is unclear. They are possibly being characterized by a lack of shame (*cf.* RSV, NIV), following the LXX but the verb usually refers to desire or longing (*cf.* Gn. 31:30; Ps. 84:2). It has been suggested that the negative particle 'not' (seen in the RSV's 'shame*less*') be understood as 'nothing', the object of the verb, referring to idols, as they are disparagingly called elsewhere (*e.g.* 2 Ki. 17:15; Jer. 2:5).[1] The people long for the aid of 'nothing' gods rather than that of the Creator of the universe (*cf.* Je. 2:11–13). This would relate the meaning to what was already stated about the people in 1:6, 12. The suggestion appears, however, to be going beyond the regular use of the particle. Although unclear, the designation is not flattering, because of the negative attitudes taken towards God's people

[1] Sabottka, pp. 62–63.

in this context.

The people are to respond quickly, because several things are imminent and soon to come, as shown by the threefold repetition of *before*, another allusion of the closeness of the Day of Yahweh (1:7, 14). Here the day is described as relating to his *anger* (*cf.* La. 2:22), his *fierce anger* (3:8; *cf.* Ex. 32:12; Is. 13:9, 13; Ho. 11:9; Na. 1:6) which *comes upon* the nation as a result of sin.

3. A positive charge is given to the *humble* (RSV, JB, NIV; 'meek', AV) *of the land*, Israel, God's chosen land and nation (*cf.* v. 1). These are the people who in poverty of spirit (*cf.* 3:12; Is. 11:4; Am. 8:4; Mt. 5:3) rely on God rather than on their own power or machinations for vindication. They are humbled in that they know that they are helpless, so they are called to *seek* three things (*cf.* the threefold repetition of 'before', v. 2). Firstly they are to seek Yahweh, their covenant God. It is his wrath and judgment that his day will bring on those who, like some in Israel, do not seek him (*cf.* 1:6). Also, in contrast to those who have abandoned him, the humble are to live godly lives, marked by 'practising justice' (*do what he commands*, NIV; *cf.* RSV, JB). In Scripture, justice is often accompanied by *righteousness* (*cf.* Is. 1:21; 9:7; Am. 5:24), which is also to be sought, as is further *humility*, submissive obedience to God (*cf.* Nu. 12:3; 2 Sa. 22:36; Ps. 45:4; Pr. 15:33). All of these positive, pious attributes are to be sought instead of the headstrong paganism which is rampant, but even then salvation, being *sheltered* from the destruction of Yahweh's wrath, is not assured. God can save, but he can also punish, so hope is held out to the pious, but it is not guaranteed. For even the most pious are among those who have broken God's law, to which they are called back, so Yahweh's decision to save is ultimately and finally a decision of grace.

The theologically significant word concerning God's help in this verse is *perhaps* (*cf.* Ex. 32:30; Am. 5:15). It could be suggested that 'perhaps' refers to the possibility of Judah's repentance and subsequent salvation, the uncertainty then being about the people's response rather than being about God. Zephaniah, however, does not seem to hold out much hope that this repentance would take place (3:7). This interpretation might be theologically more palatable, but it does not appear to be supported by the syntax of the text. God in his holiness and justice can and must punish sin; that

103

is the certainty of which his people are constantly reminded. This is not all that he is, however, or the totality of mankind would be lost. The fact that they are not destroyed arises from God's mercy, compassion and love, which are equally part of his being. Sin will lead to punishment, of that Israel could be sure, but they could also be sure that repentance and return to a covenant relationship with God would lead to their salvation and restoration (*cf.* Ex. 34:6–7; Dt. 30:1–10; Ne. 9:17; Ps. 130:4; Dn. 9:9; 1 Jn. 1:9). 'Perhaps' safeguards God's sovereign freedom, but the fullness of who he is relieves this 'perhaps' of any anxiety or uncertainty, since God, as the just Judge of all creation, can be counted on to do what is right (Gn. 18:25). From the side of man, God's forgiveness should not be misused as 'cheap grace', a guarantee against punishment for sin (*cf.* Rom. 6:1); but from God's side there is no other response possible in the face of true repentance than forgiveness. The response to God by his sinful people is commanded of them, and his response to them can safely be left in his own hands.

D. Specific scenarios of judgment (2:4 – 3:8)

i. Philistia (2:4–7). Resuming his look at judgment as it will be experienced by other nations (*cf.* 1:18), Zephaniah uses the example of what awaits the surrounding nations as a warning, giving Judah good reason to repent, as he had warned them to do (vv. 1–3). This causal connection between verses 1–3 and verses 4 to 3:8 is shown by the particle 'for' (AV, RSV, NEB; *cf.* 'yes', JB), which links these oracles against the nations with the description of the Day of Yahweh, but the force is lost due to its omission in the NIV.

4. The four principal Philistine cities are warned of impending destruction. The presentation of the first and last involves alliteration, word play based on the consonantal sounds used.[1] The four city-states are presented progressively from south to north. *Gaza, Ashkelon, Ashdod* and *Ekron* will be respectively *abandoned* (*cf.* Is. 17:9; Je. 4:29), 'laid waste' (*cf.* Lv. 26:33; Je. 4:27; 9:10), depopulated by expulsion of inhabitants (*cf.* Pss. 78:55; 80:8; Mi. 2:9) and *uprooted* (*cf.* Ec. 3:2). Ashdod's misfortune is said to take place at *midday* ('noon',

---

[1] *'azzâh 'ªzûbâh* and *'eqron tēʿaqēr*.

RSV), possibly referring to the sudden unexpectedness of its defeat in the soporific heat of the day (cf. 2 Sa. 4:5; 1 Ki. 20:16; Je. 6:4; 15:8) or to the force of the attack which would prevail in only half a day.

5. The Philistines are now addressed directly by Yahweh through the prophet. They are called *Kerethites* (cf. 1 Sa. 30:14; 2 Sa. 15:18; Ezk. 25:16), a reference to their early geographical links with Crete. Their coastal habitation (v. 6) is stressed in this oracle of *woe* (cf. Am. 5:18; 6:1; Hab. 2:9, 12, 15, 19). They are warned that they are the recipients of the *word* of Yahweh. Their destruction is sanctioned by God himself, who declares that he will bring about the annihilation of the inhabitants of Philistia. In an odd title, the *land of the Philistine* is addressed as *Canaan*. This term is usually used for the territory of the native inhabitants of the land prior to the Israelite and Philistine incursions. It is apparently also used of the southern coastal regions as well (cf. Jos. 13:3). This could be a reference to the commercial trade conducted in the region (see the commentary on 1:11).

6–7. The future of the Philistine region is described, not in terms of permanent desertion, but of reoccupation by *shepherds* and their 'folds' (RSV). The middle clause of verse 6 provides grammatical difficulties, but it appears that the *Kerethites* are again mentioned (see v. 5)[1] as possessing 'pastures' (RSV; cf. Ps. 23:2; Je. 23:3; Joel 2:22; Am. 1:2) which will be expropriated by others, namely by the *remnant* of *Judah*.

The concept of the remnant is two-sided, showing both God's holy judgment and also his gracious blessing (cf. the similar two-sided nature of the Day of Yahweh, pp. 84–85). The judgment of God against sin will be so devastating that the nation will be depleted to such an extent that only a remnant, a few battered survivors, will remain (cf. Gn. 7:23; Is. 17:6). In each of these and other examples, however, the aspect of hope is at least implicit, since the people are not completely obliterated (cf. Jos. 10:40; Je. 50:26). At least a remnant, a few battered survivors, will remain. The remnant here (cf. 1:4; 2:9; 3:13), the refugees from God's punishment, are a symbol of hope for Israel, since the promised judgment will not be total. The motif of the remnant is common in the

---

[1] There appears to have been a vowel change from *keret* resulting in assonance with the 'pastures', *i.e. nevōt kerōt*. Another root denoting digging has been suggested, resulting in 'excavations' or protective 'huts' (NEB).

prophets (*cf.* Je. 23:3; Am. 5:15; Mi. 2:12; 5:7–8), exemplifying both the severity of God's punishment and also the graciousness of his mercy. Destruction will come, but not annihilation.

The new inhabitants will also use the Philistine dwellings for accommodation (2:14; 3:13). The cause of this blessing is a beneficent 'visit' (AV; *cf.* Gn. 21:1; Je. 15:15) by Yahweh himself, Israel's faithful covenant *God*. Instead of their previous deprivation, the *fortunes* of God's people will be restored (see the commentary on 3:20).

That the passage concerning the Philistines is a unit is shown by an inclusio or envelope construction, in which an element which commences a unit is repeated at its close. In this case, the causal particle 'for' (v. 4; see p. 104), which introduces God's visit of care for Israel, also closes verse 7 (see AV, RSV, NEB, JB). The force is lost in NIV, which does not include the particle.

ii. Moab and Ammon (2:8–11). God continues to speak in the first person (see 2:5), this time directing his attention to two Transjordanian peoples. Although ethnically related to the Israelites according to the biblical narrative (see Gn. 12:4–5; 19:30–38; see p. 82), they were often in confrontation with them, either actively opposing Israel or verbally assaulting them as they do here (vv. 8, 10). Individually, the two nations are the subject of other oracles (Is. 15 – 16; Je. 48; 49:1–6; Ezk. 25:1–11; Am. 1:13 – 2:3), although never in a combined oracle as found here. The prophet also uses the oracle to declare a future universal turning to Yahweh (v. 11).

8. The wrongs of Moab and the Ammonites are spelt out (*cf.* v. 15; 3:1–4, 7), in addition to the forms of punishment which they will endure. Verbal assaults, *insults* (3:18; *cf.* Is. 25:8; 51:7; Ezk. 16:57; 36:15) and *taunts* or blasphemies (*cf.* Nu. 15:30; 2 Ki. 19:6, 22; Is. 51:7; Ezk. 5:15) are directed against Yahweh's covenant *people*, Israel (see the commentary on Hab. 3:13). The last encroachment in the verse could also be verbal, though the meaning of the clause is not clear. Literally 'they enlarged upon their border', this clause has been seen as describing territorial expansion at the expense of the Israelites (NEB), though this exact construction with a similar meaning is not found elsewhere. The construction is used elsewhere of boasting (see RSV, JB, AV; *cf.* Pss. 55:12; 138:2; Je. 48:26, 42; Ezk. 35:13), which would fit the context here, that of self-congratulation at the expense of their enemies.

9. The resulting judgment is declared with great solemnity and power. Its certainty is ensured by invoking the mighty names and titles of God as 'Yahweh of hosts', emphasizing his nature as Divine Warrior (see the commentary on Hab. 3:8–15, pp. 72–75) as well as Israel's *God*. He is therefore universal, as well as having an individual relationship with his own covenant people. His declaration is strengthened by an oath sworn upon his own life (*cf.* 1 Sa. 14:39, 45; 19:6; Is. 49:18; Je. 22:24; 46:18) that the fearsome warning will come to fruition. The punishment for these two nations will be to share the fearful destruction of *Sodom* and *Gomorrah*, the two cities near the Dead Sea which were completely destroyed for their sins (Gn. 19:24–26; *cf.* Dt. 29:23; Is. 1:9). The comparison is deliberately chosen, since the progenitors of the Moabite and Ammonite peoples were incestuously conceived in the next biblical episode after that of the destruction of the two cities (Gn. 19:30–38). The loss of previous verdure and fruitfulness is stressed by the contrast with 'nettles' (AV, RSV, JB; *weeds*, NEB, NIV; *cf.* Jb. 30:7; Pr. 24:31), *salt pits* (AV, RSV, NIV; 'heap', NEB, JB; *cf.* Ps. 65:13)[1] and eternal 'waste' (RSV, NEB). All three aspects of the comparison are drawn from the episode of the two cities: the vegetation (Gn. 19:25; Dt. 29:23), the salt (Gn. 19:26; Dt. 29:23) and the long duration of desolation (*cf.* Is. 13:19–20; Je. 50:39–40). The beneficiaries of this punishment will be those whom Moab and Ammon had scorned (see v. 8), the *remnant* (*cf.* v. 7; 3:13) and *remainder* (*cf.* Mi. 5:3; Zc. 14:2) of God's covenant *people* (v. 8). Rather than bearing the brunt of foreign incursions, the Israelites will now themselves *plunder* their enemy (*cf.* Is. 11:14; 24:3; Am. 3:11), 'dispossessing' them from their land as they did the original Canaanite inhabitants (*cf.* Gn. 15:7; 22:17; Dt. 1:8, though a different verb is used in these verses). The justice of God is here demonstrated in his elevation of the oppressed and his putting down of the oppressor.

10. The prophet himself now speaks, summarizing in prose the oracle of Yahweh which has just been given (vv. 8–9). He describes the collection of wrongs as resulting from *pride* (*cf.*

---

[1] The latter is based on the cognate Akkadian *karû* (heap), but the former fits well with the Hebrew root *kārâh*, 'dig, excavate' (*cf.* Gn. 50:5; Ps. 7:15; 40:6, AV mg.).

v. 15; Ps. 59:12; Is. 13:11; 16:6; Ezk. 16:49). The actions detailed are a reprise of verse 8, and Yahweh's name and title are taken from verse 9.

11. The oracle closes with a step back from the narrow geographical and historical focus on Moab and Ammon at this time, to encompass the rest of the world as well. The awesome might of Yahweh (*cf.* Ex. 34:10; Ps. 47:2; 66:5; 89:7) manifests itself to the Transjordanian countries when he acts against *all* their *gods*. The verb form describing what Yahweh does occurs only here, but the root seems to mean 'to cause leanness or loss' (*cf.* Is. 10:16; 17:4; Mi. 6:10). God is therefore exhibiting the gods' weakness and the diminution of their might, since ultimately he will destroy the power of their worshippers and their armies (*cf.* 3:8, 19). Not only will the gods' power be done away with, but those who worship them will now 'bow down' (RSV) to Yahweh. They, the very pagan nations in their furthest 'regions' (*land*, RSV, NIV), will worship him, each from his own place of habitation. This could mean that foreigners will flock to Jerusalem (*cf.* Is. 2:3; Mi. 4:1; Zc. 14:16), or that Yahweh-worship will no longer be tied geographically or ethnically to one place and people, but all will recognize him (see 3:9). There is a structural parallel at the close of each half of the verse (see AV, RSV), in which the totality ('all') of the doomed gods are in contrast with the universal ('all') extent of the worship of the true God.

iii. Cush (2:12). Moving to the south of Israel, the next oracle concerns the *Cushites* or Ethiopians. This is probably a reference to Egypt, one of the two major powers, who had herself been subject in the late eighth and early seventh centuries BC to the Ethiopian Twenty-fifth Dynasty (see pp. 82–83; *cf.* 3:10; Is. 11:11; 18; 20:3–6). It could, however, refer to the defeat of Egypt by Cambyses II of Persia in 525 BC. If it refers to Ethiopia rather than Egypt, we know that Cambyses also campaigned in Upper Egypt during the same period. This nation, directly addressed here by Yahweh, will meet military destruction, death (*cf.* Nu. 19:18; Is. 22:2; Je. 14:18) by Yahweh's own *sword* (*cf.* Is. 34:5–6; 66:16).

iv. Assyria (2:13–15). 13. Turning *north* now, Yahweh acts against the second major power of the period, *Assyria*, and its capital *Nineveh* (*cf.* Nahum). In a gesture of judgment, Yahweh resolves to *stretch out his hand* (see 1:4 and references) in order to *destroy* them (*cf.* v. 5; Dt. 11:4; Pss. 5:6; 21:10; Is. 26:14). Even their mighty city Nineveh (*cf.* Jon. 1:2; 3:3) will become a 'desolation' (RSV; *cf.* vv. 9, 15) and revert to an arid wilderness (*cf.* Ps. 63:1; Je. 2:6; 50:12; 51:43; Joel 2:20).

14. The utter desolation is stressed by enumerating some of the city's occupants. These will include domestic *flocks* (*cf.* Gn. 32:19; Ps. 78:52; Is. 40:11) and wild *creatures* ('beasts', RSV), a textually difficult form.[1] The two groups are apparently meant to comprise the totality of the animal realm, both domestic and wild (*cf.* Gn. 1:24; Ps. 50:10). These earthbound creatures are joined by the inhabitants of the sky in the rest of the verse.

The *columns*, the pillar tops of the destroyed buildings' walls (*cf.* Am. 9:1), will become the roosting place of birds. While the exact identities of the birds are disputed ('cormorant', AV; 'horned owl', NEB; 'vulture', RSV; 'pelican', JB; *desert owl*, NIV; *cf.* Lv. 11:18; Dt. 14:17; Ps. 102:6; 'bittern', AV; 'hedgehog', RSV; 'ruffed bustard', NEB; 'heron', JB; *screech owl*, NIV; *cf.* Is. 14:23), both are elsewhere associated with desertion and lack of human habitation (*cf.* Is. 14:23; 34:11). The desolation is emphasized by a particle before each word, showing that 'even' (JB; 'both', AV; but omitted by the RSV, NEB, NIV) these two birds, which would not in ordinary circumstances be city-dwellers, will be in this now deserted place. A 'call', probably of the birds, 'trills' ('hoot', RSV, NEB, JB; 'sing', AV; *cf.* 2 Ch. 29:28). The buildings themselves are so much *rubble* ('desolation', AV; *cf.* Is. 61:4; Je. 49:13; Ezk. 29:10),[2] from the 'thresholds' of the doors (AV; *cf.* Jdg. 19:27; Is. 6:4; Ezk. 40:6) to the *beams of cedar* (*cf.* Nu. 24:6; Is. 41:19) of the walls or ceilings, which will be *exposed* due to the destruction and the

---

[1] Lit. 'beasts of the nation (*gôy*)', there is an apparent misreading, *ge'*, 'valley' or 'field' (*cf.* LXX, RSV, JB; see J. Barr, *Comparative Philology and the Text of the Old Testament* [Oxford University Press, 1968], pp. 144, 324). Synonymous phrases, *e.g.* 'beast of the field' or 'earth', are common (*cf.* Gn. 1:24–25, 30; 2:19–20; 3:1). The NIV renders the construction 'creatures of every kind', apparently an attempt to make some sense of the difficult text, but without readily apparent textual support.

[2] The LXX, followed by the RSV and JB (*cf.* NEB), reads 'raven' for 'rubble', an alteration of one letter which could easily have occurred if the text was copied by dictation. The bird would fit the larger context of the verse, but its association with the lower post of a door frame is problematic.

lack of maintenance. This sort of abandonment to nature is not uncommon for those who oppose God (*cf.* Is. 13:19–22; 34:11–15; Je. 50:39).[1]

15. The reason for the fall from might of this one-time 'exultant' (RSV; NEB; *cf.* 3:11; Is. 22:2; 23:7) and 'secure' (RSV) city (*cf.* 3:2; Lv. 25:18–19; Is. 47:8; Je. 23:6; Zc. 14:11) is its arrogant pride, thinking itself (*cf.* 1:12) as without peer (Is. 47:8, 10; *cf.* Zp. 3:11). Her insolent claim of self-sufficiency and uniqueness would place Assyria in opposition to the very first of God's ten words to Israel (Ex. 20:3), who was commanded to have Yahweh alone as her God. Nineveh was arrogating this position to herself, usurping a privilege reserved for God alone. Like the coming Babylonian king (see Is. 14:3–23, esp. v. 14), prideful Nineveh will be obliterated. The prophet exclaims in amazement at the fall and degradation visible in the great city which has become a 'waste' (NEB; *ruin*, JB, NIV; *cf.* 1:13; 2:4, 9, 13; Is. 5:9; Mi. 6:16) and a beast's *lair* (*cf.* v. 14; Ezk. 25:5). Even the ordinary passers-by react in scorn and amazement, making sounds ('whistle', JB; 'hiss', AV, RSV, NEB; Je. 19:8; La. 2:15–16; Ezk. 27:36) and motions, shaking their hands.[2] This mention of the hand forms an inclusio, opening and closing this oracle (*cf.* p. 106). The message starts with God's hand raised in judgment and closes with a hand raised in amazement at the judgment wrought.

v. Jerusalem (3:1–7). As a rhetorical device, the prophet would gradually get to the heart of his message of judgment by first dealing with the neighbouring peoples. The audience would agree that they deserved what God was giving them, so they would not be prepared for the recitation of their own faults as well (*cf.* Am. 1:3 – 2:16). Now the time is rhetorically ripe to confront God's own people, Judah, and their capital, Jerusalem, with their sin (vv. 1–4), shamelessness (v. 5) and lack of repentance (vv. 6–7).

a. Sins compounded (3:1–5). The identity of the city mourned

---

[1] See D. Hillers, 'Treaty-Curses and the Old Testament Prophets', *Biblica et Orientalia* 16 (Rome, 1964), pp. 44–54.

[2] The ordinary action in response to sights such as this is a shake of the head (*cf.* Pss. 22:7; 109:25; Is. 37:22; La. 2:15). Rather than a motion of aggression (*cf.* JB, NIV), a motion of commiseration or scorn seems to fit the context better here.

in this dirge (*cf.* 2:5) is not explicit. The preceding context would suggest that Nineveh is still being referred to, so Israel would have continued in agreement with God's oracles of judgment against this city. This type of rhetorical device brings the message home by having the audience identifying with it by agreeing with its content. It is rhetorically powerful because the hearers soon realize that it is *not* after all Nineveh which is being condemned, but rather Jerusalem, their own capital, and that not their enemy but they themselves are being judged by God. The lack of response to Yahweh (v. 2), who is Israel's God and not Assyria's, and who is closely associated with the condemned city (v. 5), supports the suggested identification of Jerusalem as the city referred to here. This is also supported by the similarity of literary structure with Amos 1:3 – 2:16. There also God's own people, the primary target of the condemnation, are presented last in a series of oracles against the nations, and thus serve as the climax of the passage.

1. Jerusalem, rather than being God's faithful, covenant city in contrast to her pagan neighbours, is in fact one with them in her sinfulness and unfaithfulness (*cf.* Is. 1:21). She is addressed in a lament (*cf.* Je. 22:18; 34:5) as her fate is sealed because of her rebelliousness (*cf.* Je. 4:17; 5:23; Ho. 14:1), defilement (*cf.* Is. 59:3; 63:3; Mal. 1:7, 12) and oppressive brutality (*cf.* Je. 25:38; 46:16; 50:16).

2. The indictment continues by showing further sins of the city as a whole, including lack of obedience (lit. 'listening to the voice'; *cf.* 1 Sa. 8:7; Je. 3:13) and rejection of discipline (v. 7; Je. 2:30; 5:3; 7:28). Yahweh, the God who entered into covenant with his people to enjoy a unique relationship with them (*cf.* Ex. 19:5–6; Dt. 4:7, 31), is now rejected by his people. They show mistrust (*cf.* 2 Ki. 18:5; Pss. 13:5; 25:2; 26:1; Is. 26:4) and distance themselves from him by not serving and worshipping him as they ought (*cf.* Ezk. 44:15).

3–4. Civil and religious leaders within the city are also charged with actions incompatible with their positions. The two civil leadership categories, *officials* (RSV, NIV; 1:8; Je. 2:26) and 'judges' (AV, RSV, JB) are compared to wild animals, *lions* (*cf.* Jdg. 14:5; Pr. 28:15; Am. 3:8; Na. 2:12) and *wolves* 'of the evening' (*cf.* Gn. 49:27; Is. 11:6; Je. 5:6; see the commentary on Hab. 1:8), both known for their merciless ferocity (*cf.* esp. Ezk. 22:25, 27). Rather than protecting and leading the flock which is entrusted to them, the leaders devour the people for their own gain (*cf.* Is. 56:11; Je. 23:1; Ezk. 34:2). They do their work so well that there are not even bones left to 'gnaw' (AV; Nu. 24:8; *cf.* Gn. 49:14; Pr. 17:22)[1] by *morning*, a time associated with legal judgment and justice (v. 5; *cf.* 2 Sa. 15:2; Ps. 101:8; Je. 21:12).

The religious leaders are no better. The *prophets* are supposed to be the intermediaries between God and man, accurately and unflinchingly presenting the divine will. Rather than basing their words on the sure and faithful foundation of God's revelation, they speak words of their own which have no more solid foundation than do the tossing sea waters (Gn. 49:4; *cf.* Jdg. 9:4; Je. 23:32). The faithful words of Yahweh are replaced by *treacherous* words of lying men (*cf.* Is. 24:16; Je. 3:20). The *priests*, on the other hand, were responsible for representing man before God through presenting sacrifices, as well as for teaching God's law to the people (*cf.* Lv. 1–7; Dt. 17:8–13; 21:5). They flagrantly perverted both of these charges. Rather than sanctifying the people through the sacrifical rituals, they *profane*, or made unsuitable for the holy God (*cf.* Lv. 10:10; 19:8; Ezk. 20:13), that which was 'the holy', most probably a reference to the Temple (AV, NEB, NIV; *cf.* 2 Ch. 29:7; Is. 43:28; Dn. 8:13; Mal. 2:11). Rather than keeping the *law* or instruction of God (*cf.* Is. 30:9; 42:21, 24) and instructing others in it, they violated and perverted it (*cf.* Ezk. 22:26). All who should have led God's people in just and holy living were instead leading them astray.

5. Yahweh is also *within* the city (*cf.* v. 3), but his character and actions are in contradistinction to its leaders' (vv. 1–4). In particular, his righteousness, which is explained as a lack of 'wrongdoing' (v. 13; *cf.* Mi. 3:10; Hab. 2:12; Mal. 2:6), is contrasted with their misbehaviour. His *justice*, too, is continually and dependably disclosed (*cf.* La. 3:22–23; Ho. 6:3).

---

[1] The exact meaning of the clause indicating the rulers' actions is unclear due to the rarity of the verbal root (*grm*) used. Though there might be some textual corruption (see W. L. Holladay, *A Concise Hebrew and Aramaic Lexicon of the Old Testament* [Wm B. Eerdmans, 1971], p. 64), there is no major manuscript evidence for emendation (*cf. BHS*, note a., adopted and modified by the NIV). The other contexts in which the root occurs do indicate an association with bones, so the proposed interpretation has merit.

Yahweh himself is infallible and lacks nothing (*cf.* 2 Sa. 17:22; Is. 40:26), never guilty of a miscarriage of justice, as opposed to the 'wrongdoer' (*cf.* 'wrongdoing' earlier in this verse; Jb. 18:21; 27:7; 31:3) who never experiences *shame* (v. 19; *cf.* Is. 30:3, 5; Je. 2:26; Hab. 2:10). In all of the points where the city's appointed leaders were derelict in character or in fulfilling their duty, Yahweh, their overlord, is faithful in his being and actions. In spite of Israel's disregard of their promise to maintain a monogamous relationship with God alone (see 1:4-6), Yahweh remains committed to his people. He is there in their very capital city, even though they no longer acknowledge him.

b. Demonstration ignored (3:6-7). Yahweh is not characterized by capriciousness or by eagerness to punish his own people. He acted against the pagan nations (v. 6; *cf.* 2:4-15) as an example and a warning to his own people and city. This aspect of God's character, longsuffering and a willingness to delay or withhold punishment, is not rare in the Bible (*cf.* Ex. 34:6-7; Nu. 14:18-19; Am. 4:6-11; 7:1-6; Rom. 9:22-24). This warning the people wilfully chose to ignore. Both history and current events show signs of God's displeasure with sin, but the lessons are not learnt.

6. Yahweh himself speaks, detailing his forceful actions against the *nations*[1] and *their cities* which had not acknowledged him as God. The verbs used are powerful, indicating major destruction (*cut off*, 1:3-4; 3:7; *cf.* Am. 1:5; Mi. 5:9; Zc. 9:6; 'ruined', 1:13; 2:4, 9, 13, 15; *cf.* Joel 1:17; Am. 7:9; *left* . . . *deserted*, Jdg. 16:24; 2 Ki. 19:17; Is. 42:15; 'been sacked',[2] JB; *cf. destroyed*, AV, NIV). The objects of destruction are presented as animate – *nations*, passers-by and inhabitants, as well as inanimate – *cities*, *streets* (*cf.* Am. 5:16; Na. 3:10; Zc. 10:5) and defensive corner emplacements (1:16; *cf.* Is. 28:16; Je. 51:26; Zc. 10:4). All will be brought to nought.

7. The city (vv. 1-5) is called upon to worship Yahweh by fearing (2:11; *cf.* Gn. 22:12; Ps. 55:19; Is. 25:3; 59:19; Mal. 2:5; see Zp. 3:15-16) or living in awe of him. This is not to be

---

[1] The NEB reads 'proud', following the LXX reading which arises from a difference of one letter. The Heb. text is perfectly understandable as it stands and the proposed emendation is not compelling.

[2] This is the sole OT use of this word, so the meaning is derivable only from its use in the present context and is therefore tentative.

simply an emotional reaction, but is to involve behavioural change through accepting *correction* (v. 2; Pr. 1:3; 15:33) or renewing obedience to God (*cf.* Ps. 111:10; Pr. 1:7). If the right response were given, the city would *not be cut off* (*cf.* v. 6) from its *dwelling* place. This is in explicit contrast to the fate of the pagans when God visits them for *punishment* (*cf.* Jb. 35:15; Je. 5:9). But this possibility was not to be, for not even the recent and adjacent catastrophe affecting Israel had the desired impact upon Judah.

Contrary to the hoped-for ready, positive response to Yahweh, the people were eager to continue their corruption (*cf.* Dt. 4:16; Ps. 14:1; Is. 1:4). This was shown in all of their 'deeds' (RSV; v. 11; *cf.* Ps. 99:8). Grace is offered, but frivolously spurned, a sobering epitaph for the city of David.

vi. The world (3:8). In a climactic 'oracle', Yahweh promises a cataclysmic end to all inhabitants of the earth. *Therefore*, he says, in view of their decision to rebel (v. 7), the people are told to *wait* for Yahweh. Often this verb has a positive connotation of expected blessing (*cf.* Ps. 33:20; Is. 8:17; 30:18; Mi. 7:7). While this is what the people might anticipate, it is not what will be forthcoming. The prophet has taken a familiar phrase and turned it on its head in a powerful rhetorical device, bringing the point home to the audience. The *day* will come when Yahweh will arise (RSV) in wrath and judgment (*cf.* Ps. 76:9; Is. 2:19, 21) in order *to testify* against all people ('accuse', NEB, JB; 'as a witness', RSV; 'to the prey', AV;[1] *cf.* Je. 29:23; 42:5; Mi. 1:2; Mal. 3:5). Yahweh's just 'decision' (RSV; 2:3; 3:15 [*mišpaṭ*, meaning 'legal decision' being used in each verse]) is *to gather* (vv. 18–20; Is. 66:18; Joel 3:2; Mi. 4:12; Mt. 25:32) all of the *nations* together. This is in order to mete out his judgment upon them and to *pour out* (1:17) his 'indignation' (AV, RSV, NEB; *cf.* Is. 10:5, 25; 30:27; La. 2:6) and *anger* (2:2; *cf.* La. 4:11). In a refrain echoing the conclusion of the description of the judgment on the Day of Yahweh (1:18), these scenarios close with *fire* consuming the earth (see the commentary on 1:18). In both general (1:8–18) and specific

---

[1] The MT, followed by the AV, reads *l^eʿad*, 'plunder' (*cf.* Gn. 49:27; Is. 33:23). This does not fit the context of the passage, in which Yahweh does not plunder, but destroys. The reading adopted here, following the LXX, fits much better into this forensic context, and requires only a change in Heb. vocalization.

cases (2:4 – 3:8), the depravity of man can be met only by the wrath of God, since an integral part of his character is holiness and the inability to countenance sin.

E. The nature of the day – hope (3:9–20)

While Yahweh's character includes holiness, justice, righteousness and an intolerance of sin (*cf.* v. 8), it also includes grace, love and forgiveness. Fiery judgment will be meted out justly upon all peoples, but not for their total annihilation (v. 8). Rather it will be for the purification (v. 9) of the nations (vv. 9–10). A righteous remnant of God's own people will remain after the dross of sin and rebellion has been removed (vv. 11–13). The prophet summons the people to rejoice in this grace (vv. 14–17), which is wrought solely by Yahweh himself (vv. 18–20).

i. Nations converted (3:9–10). 9. In contrast to his roles as judge and bailiff, carrying out the decreed punishment (v. 8), Yahweh takes on a new role as saviour. *Then*, pursuant to and resulting from the smelting process of his judgment, he will 'transform' ('change', RSV), the *lips* ('speech', RSV) of the *peoples* (1:4; 3:12,19–20), purifying them (*cf.* Jb. 33:3) as God's seraph cleansed Isaiah (Is. 6:5–7). This could be seen as a reversal of Babel (*cf.* Gn. 11:1, 6–7, 9),[1] with a common language replacing a plurality of tongues. The context appears better to support a theological interpretation than an anthropological one. Unity is portrayed not as that of form, but rather of function. The purpose of the purification, as that of Isaiah's cleansing, is to address God appropriately. It is to *call* on Yahweh's *name* (*cf.* Gn. 4:26; 1 Ch. 16:8; Ps. 105:1; Is. 12:4) in worship and service (*cf.* Ex. 10:26; Nu. 8:11; Jos. 24:14–15,18–19, 21–22). This service will not only be in unity, *shoulder to shoulder* (*cf.* similar phrases with different body parts in 1 Ki. 22:13; Je. 32:39), but it will also be universal, since *all* peoples will take part. The purpose of the punishment, not only of Judah but of all the nations, is restoration for all, conversion of the pagans to Yahweh. Strife and enmity will disappear, and harmony and peace and shared worship of Yahweh will result (*cf.* 1 Ki. 8:41–43; Pss. 22:27; 102:22;

---

[1] *Cf.* Craigie, p. 128.

Is. 2:2–4; 56:1–7; Mal. 1:11).

10. The geographical diversity of the peoples who will turn to God (v. 9) is accentuated by describing one such group from the Upper Nile (*rivers of Cush*; *cf.* Is. 18:1; Zp. 2:12). They will bring God *offerings* (*cf.* Gn. 4:3; Ps. 72:10; Ho. 10:6). These people are described as those who pray to God ('suppliants', AV, RSV, NEB, JB; *cf.* Gn. 25:21; Ex. 8:30; Jb. 33:26), indicating their conversion to him as lord and provider. They are scattered and dispersed (*cf.* Gn. 11:4; Nu. 10:35; Zc. 13:7), once geographically separate from the centre of God's gracious actions in the promised land. Even the Ethiopians are under his sovereign care, and he calls them 'mine' (*cf.* Is. 18:7; 19:18–25; 45:14; Acts 8:26–39).

ii. The remnant preserved (3:11–13). Speaking more specifically again to Jerusalem and its inhabitants (vv. 1–7), Yahweh proffers them hope in spite of their sin. Impure elements will be removed from the nation (*cf.* v. 9) so that a righteous remnant will remain.

11. *That day*, the Day of Yahweh, brought punishment and ignominy due to the sins of God's people (1:7–10, 14–15). This is not the end, however, since the day is also a time of hope and help. The *shame* of Jerusalem (*cf.* vv. 5,19; Is. 54:4; Joel 2:26–27) will not continue in spite of previous 'misdeeds' (JB; v. 7). To neutralize these, Yahweh himself will 'expel' (v. 15; *cf.* 1 Sa. 17:26; 2 Ki. 18:4, 22; Ezk. 11:19) the troublemakers, the 'proud boasters' (JB; 2:15; Is. 13:11; Je. 48:29). The Temple mount, God's *holy hill* (*cf.* Is. 2:2; Joel 2:1; Ob. 16) will thus be free from haughtiness and *pride* (*cf.* Is. 3:16; Ezk. 28:2,17), one of the major sins involved in an endeavour to live without God.

12. Instead of being arrogant (v. 11), those left (the 'remnant', 1:4; 2:7, 9; 3:13) among God's people will be the 'humble' (RSV, JB; 2:3; Matt. 5:3; Lk. 6:20) and 'lowly' (RSV, JB; Am. 2:7; 8:4). Poverty is thus seen here not as a judgment from God, but rather as an indicator of Yahweh's special covenant love and care for the impoverished ones. They can *trust* (AV, NIV; Ps. 2:12; 22:8; 57:1) in the power of his *name* (v. 9; *cf.* Ps. 20:1; Pr. 18:10; Ho. 12:5; Acts 2:21; Phil. 2:9–10). He will continue to sustain them even though they have lived in the midst of a sinful people.

13. This *remnant* ('those left', v. 12) will share characteristics with Yahweh himself, in contrast to their sinful brothers, in that *no wrong* will be done (v. 5) and their words will not be false (*cf.* Je. 9:2–8; Ezk. 13:6–8). Pure words of worship to Yahweh (v. 9) will replace reliance on pagan deities (1:5). Blasphemy and *deceit* (*cf.* Ps. 119:118; Je. 8:5; 14:14) will be non-existent. Faith will result in ethical works. As a benefit of humble faithfulness, instead of want and strife there will be pasturage (2:7; *cf.* Mi. 7:14; Zc. 11:7) and 'rest' (JB; 2:7,14; Ps. 23:2) free from fear (*cf.* Lv. 26:6; Je. 30:10; Mi. 4:4; Na. 2:11). When the Creator is worshipped and served as he ought to be, paradise is regained.

iii. A psalm of joy (3:14–17). Putting himself into the time in the future when the remnant will be blessed, or in confident anticipation of that blessing, the author summons God's people to rejoice. In a form similar to other psalms of salvation (*cf.* Ps. 98; Is. 12:1–6; 52:7–10), the prophet commands praise (v. 14) not only for what Yahweh has done in the past (v. 15a), and also for future deliverance (v. 17), but for the very presence of Yahweh in the midst of the nation as the loving king who inspires confidence (vv. 15–17).

This self-contained little psalm (see pp. 87–88) could have been written by Zephaniah for this prophecy, or it could have been adopted from its previous use in the liturgy of God's people as a fitting response to Yahweh's grace bestowed once again upon his people. It continues the motif of God's continued presence in Zion, the city of David, as promised in the covenant in 2 Samuel 7 and picked up in Isaiah and some psalms (*e.g.* Pss. 2; 89).[1]

14–15. In a tripartite example of synonymous parallelism, where the same idea is repeated three times in different words, God's people are called to *sing* (*cf.* v. 17; Is. 54:1; Zc. 2:10), *shout* (*cf.* Is. 44:23; Ho. 5:8; Zc. 9:9) and joyfully 'exult' (RSV). This is not to be due to their own proud actions (*cf.* 2:15; 3:11), but because of what Yahweh has done in delivering them (v. 11) from their unspecified *enemy* as well as from the *punishment* ('judgments', AV, RSV; 2:3; 3:8; *cf.* 1 Ki. 20:40) which was their due. God's people are described in three ways, two geographical and one ethnic. They are described in terms

[1] See J. Bright, *Covenant and Promise* (SCM Press/Westminster, 1977), esp. pp. 49–77, 94–110.

of *Zion*, David's city (v. 16; *cf.* 2 Sa. 5:7; Is. 1:8; 10:32; see p. 83), and *Jerusalem*,[1] names apparently antedating David's period. Ethnically they are called *Israel*, after the progenitor of the people (Gn. 28:10–15; 32:28). Each name would recall to the hearers a period of significant activity on the part of Yahweh in the life of his people.

Two additional causes for rejoicing are enumerated. The first is the presence of *the King of Israel*, Yahweh, in the very 'midst' (AV, RSV, JB, *cf.* NEB; *with you*, NIV) of his people (vv. 5, 17; *cf.* 2 Sa. 7:9). Rather than being absent or impotent, as claimed by some (*cf.* 1:12), Yahweh is the sovereign covenant God of Israel. He is the God who is there. As a result of his benevolent presence, there is no need for more *fear* (vv. 7, 16).[2] 'Evil' (AV, RSV, JB), which had previously been a cause for concern, will now be shown to be powerless before Yahweh. Enemies (*cf.* 2 Sa. 7:1; Ps. 89:42, 51) will be repulsed and God's punishment on the people will be 'removed' (*cf.* 2 Sa. 7:15, where the same verb is used in the original context of God's eternal covenant with David and Zion).

16–17. The prophet now refers the people back to *that day*, the Day of Yahweh which had previously been painted as a day of judgment and doom (*cf.* the commentary on v. 11 and the references there). Now he says that as a result of God's grace to the humble who follow him (v. 12), *fear* and its physiological manifestation, powerlessness (lit. 'limp hands'; *cf.* Is. 13:7; Je. 6:24; 50:43), should not be experienced.

The reason for this fearless confidence is the presence of Yahweh, now described as Israel's *God* as well as her king (v. 15). He acts mightily as a heroic saviour (1:14; 3:19; *cf.* Ex. 14:30; Is. 9:6). As the Divine Warrior led Israel out of bondage and through the conquest of the promised land (*cf.* Dt. 4:34; Jos. 4:24; Jdg. 6:12), so his same power is still available to Israel in its need, as it is to the church (*cf.* Ps. 24:8; Is. 9:6; 10:21; Mk. 9:1; 2 Cor. 10:4). Yahweh also reacts as an abandoned parent or a jilted lover to whom the beloved has returned. He responds in joy (*cf.* Is. 62:5; 65:19; Lk. 15:11–32). This involves both vocal jubilation (v. 14; *cf.* Is. 54:1; 55:12) and stillness and *quiet* (*cf.* Jb. 11:3) in the presence of such

[1] See *NBD*, pp. 566–572.
[2] The reading 'you will not see', supported by the LXX and Syr., is not compelling. The present MT verb 'fear' occurs in the next verse in a concentric construction (see p. 87) which would be lost if the word were emended.

love. The battle cry on the day of judgment (1:14) will be replaced by the poignant hush of the reuniting of two lovers.

iv. God's promise (3:18–20). The prophecy does not end with the people's joyful response to God's goodness (vv. 14–17), but with further blessings promised by God. There will be relief from oppression, separation and suffering, all of which are to be replaced by repatriation, acclaim and plenty.

18. This verse's textual obscurity is reflected by the diversity of its translation. The first phrase concerns 'festivals' (RSV, JB), special days of fixed periodicity in the Hebrew religious calendar (*cf.* Gn. 1:14; Lev. 23:2, 4; Ezk. 46:9, 11; Ho. 2:11; 9:5; 12:9). The LXX links these with verse 17 (*cf.* also RSV, JB), reflecting the ritual situations in which God's joyful presence would be experienced. This understanding restores the two-part structure of each Hebrew line in verses 17–18, which was broken by the present verse division. (If the chiasm or concentric parallelism proposed for vv. 14–17 is valid [see pp. 87–88], this verse is not part of the unit since it falls outside this structure.) It also appears to ignore the first word of this verse, which apparently denotes *sorrows* (*cf.* La. 1:4) for or on account of these feasts.[1] The mournful would be incongruous in the context of the joy of verse 17, but they find a better home in the more sombre environment of the verse in which they are presently found.

The final two nouns in the verse concern a *burden* (AV, NIV; *cf.* Am. 5:11, AV), or heaping up of difficulty occasioned by the *reproach* (AV, RSV, NEB, NIV; *cf.* commentary on 2:8 and the references there) or 'disgrace' (JB) experienced by God's people. This possibly arose from the previous neglect of ritual obligations such as the established holy days just mentioned.

The two phrases are separated by two verbs. The first suggests most clearly a *gathering* by God (AV, NASB; *cf.* the commentary on v. 8 and the references there) of the sorrowful, but the purpose of such an action in this jubilant context is not spelt out and is not clear. Reading instead a verbal form signifying *removal* (RSV, JB, NIV; *cf.* the commentary on 1:2 and the references there) of the sorrow and shame links the

---

[1] A possible occurrence of the same root in a different verbal form, signifying 'thrust away, carry off' (2 Sa. 20:13), referring here to those who have abandoned or neglected these festivals, has been proposed by R. L. Smith, p. 143.

verse with its larger context of joy in God. The sorrows are said to arise *from you*, that is, from God's own people who are being addressed (vv. 15, 17, 19–20), but their dispersion is from God. The faithful and true Yahweh-worshippers can thus be encouraged that meaningful observance will be restored.

19–20. God's gracious intervention is imminent. An adverb expresses the immediate, 'here and now' (JB; *cf.* Gn. 6:17; Ex. 10:4; Je. 30:10) aspect of his dealings (*cf.* Ezk. 22:14; 23:25; Mi. 5:15 [Heb. v. 14]) with those who have, until this point, been afflicting (*cf.* Gn. 16:6; Jdg. 16:5; Is. 60:14) God's people. Whether internal opponents of God and his people (*cf.* Ne. 4:10, 12; 5:1–2) or their external enemies (*cf.* Ne. 4:1, 3, 7, 11; 6:1–2), all will find themselves under the control of Yahweh.

Specific benefits are mentioned that will arise for God's covenant people *at that time*. Those disadvantaged, either by physical disability, such as the *lame* (Mi. 4:6–7; *cf.* Gn. 32:32), or by geographical or social dispossession and statelessness, the *scattered* ('outcast', RSV; *cf.* Dt. 30:4; Je. 40:12; 43:5; Mi. 4:6), will experience the blessing of God's active *rescue* (NEB, JB, NIV; v. 17), and his gathering (vv. 8, 20; *cf.* Mi. 4:6) of them to himself and his care. The rejected are restored and the cripples receive care. In every situation in which these unfortunates had been shamed (v. 5) and reproached, their lot will be reversed. Instead of being a byword, they will be objects of *praise* (v. 20) and *honour* (1:4; 3:9, 12, 20; *cf.* Dt. 26:19; Je. 13:11; 33:9). This is not through their own merit, but because of the actions of God.

The gathering and honouring are reiterated and their application is expanded in the closing verse of the prophecy. *At that* same *time*, Yahweh will *bring* his people. This is explained as restoring them to their former position. At times the clause is used of a restoration from captivity (*cf.* Je. 29:14), which would fit the linguistic context of the passage (*cf. bring you home*). The more general idea of *restore the fortunes* (see 2:7, *cf.* Jb. 42:10; Ezk. 16:53) would perhaps be more suitable here. The whole passage is concerned with the restoration of good rather than with some release from captivity.

The blessings are sure and the promises can and will be fulfilled because it is Yahweh himself, the covenant-keeping God, who delivers them. The message of repentance and hope thus ends as it began, with the identification of its divine source as Yahweh (1:1; see p. 88).